Success

Learn and Practise

KS3 English

Nick Barber

Contents

Contents

Varying sentences for effect 1

Writing

Learn

Sentence parts

There are a number of parts within a sentence. The main part of a sentence is called the main clause. Other clauses are called subordinate clauses.

Here is an example of a sentence with a main clause and a subordinate clause:

Jim played the guitar, *because he was in a band*.

    ↑   ↑

Main clause   *Subordinate clause*

If you change the order of the main clause and the subordinate clause, you can create a different emphasis in the sentence:

Because he was in a band, **Jim played the guitar**.

    ↑   ↑

Subordinate clause   **Main clause**

By leaving the main clause until the end of the sentence, greater tension is created, because the reader does not know what the main reason for the sentence is straightaway.

Sentences with more than two clauses

Many sentences have more than two clauses. These sentences can be arranged in a variety of ways, creating different emphasis. Look at these examples:

Billy played the mandolin, *despite his age*, <u>because he enjoyed it</u>.

    ↑   ↑   ↑

Main clause   *Subordinate clause 1*   <u>Subordinate clause 2</u>

<u>Because he enjoyed it</u>, **Billy played the mandolin**, *despite his age*.

    ↑   ↑   ↑

<u>Subordinate clause 2</u>   **Main clause**   *Subordinate clause 1*

When writing, therefore, it is best to try different variations of the same sentence, in order to see which works best. When you write, consider which part of the sentence you want to emphasise, or whether you want to build up tension or create surprise.

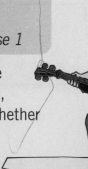

Key words   main clause • subordinate clause

Sentence parts

1 Circle the main clause and <u>underline</u> the subordinate clause in each of these sentences.

a) Becky didn't do her homework, because she had lost her book.

b) Sadie said that she understood the work, even though it was difficult.

c) Despite being well behaved, Alex was told off by the teacher.

d) Although she had been away, Laura got top marks in the exam.

e) Sara laughed, because Sophie dropped her sweets.

f) Emily's work was good, despite being untidy.

g) Because she had a cold, Courtney was absent.

2 Rewrite the sentences above, but change the order of the clauses in each sentence.

a) _____

b) _____

c) _____

d) _____

e) _____

f) _____

g) _____

14

Sentences with more than two clauses

1 <u>Underline</u> the subordinate clauses in each of these sentences.

a) Although he was very young, Grant was a great musician, who many admired.

b) Mike loved painting, because it gave him an extra income, alongside his teaching job.

c) Although his children didn't like it, Gerald's beard grew, because he didn't shave.

2 Re-write the sentences above, but put the clauses in a different order. There are several possible ways of doing this.

a) _____

b) _____

c) _____

6

Practise

Writing

Total marks   20

5

Varying sentences for effect 2

Writing

Learn

Short sentences

Different sentence lengths can be used to create different effects. There are no hard and fast rules for what is right or wrong when using sentence lengths, but there are some general ways in which you might create different sentences for different purposes.

Short sentences may be **simple sentences** (i.e. with a subject and a verb) or **sentence fragments**. Short sentences can be used:
- To create impact, e.g. Really?
- As part of speech, for example when someone is shouting, e.g. "Stop it! Now!"
- To make a point, e.g. That *is* the answer.
- To create suspense or tension, e.g. They walked slowly. The door was shut. It was silent.
- To give instructions or commands, e.g. Open the box. Take the money. Spend it wisely.
- To make your ideas clearer, e.g. The gears rotate. They then power the engine.

Note how in some of these examples, the rule about a sentence needing a verb and a subject is sometimes broken deliberately for effect.

Long sentences

Long sentences may be **compound sentences** or **complex sentences** (i.e. with more than one clause). Long sentences can be used:
- To create descriptive detail, e.g. Vince pushed at the door gingerly and stepped forward nervously – like a frightened little boy – into the dark, sullen interior, wondering what secrets he would uncover.
- To add extra information, e.g. Before you cook the steak, ensure that the oven has been heated to the right cooking temperature, so that the meat spends the correct amount of time in the oven.
- To create tension or suspense, e.g. There, high on the hill, surrounded by trees and rarely visited by humankind, stood the house in which very strange things had happened – the place where he dared not go.
- To create the impression of intelligence, e.g. If, like some people, you find yourself unable to get things right first time, you ought to follow the rules set out by the teacher. (*Be careful with this – sometimes, using long sentences can make the writer seem pompous!*).
- To build up to a final idea, e.g. If, instead of spending their money on electrical goods, junk food, new clothes and trips to the cinema, they had saved sensibly with their earnings, they might have had enough money left over to go on holiday.

Key words   purpose • subject • verb • command

Short sentences

1 Write an example of a short sentence for each of the following purposes:

a) To create impact. _____

b) As part of speech. _____

c) To make a point. _____

d) To create suspense or tension. _____

e) To write instructions or give commands.

_____

f) To make your ideas clearer. _____

6

Long sentences

1 Write an example of a long sentence for each of the following purposes:

a) To create descriptive detail.

_____

_____

b) To add extra information.

_____

_____

c) To create tension or suspense.

_____

_____

d) To create the impression of intelligence.

_____

_____

e) To build up to a final idea.

_____

_____

5

Total marks 11

Punctuation 1

At Level 6, a range of punctuation has to be used in a consistent and accurate manner. This means that your writing has to include more than full stops and commas.

Semi-colons

A semi-colon (;) marks a long gap or pause in a sentence. In terms of the length of pause, it is sometimes described as being between a comma and a colon.

Semi-colons are used between clauses that could exist on their own, but which are closely related or linked, for example:

> He couldn't do the exam; he had forgotten his pen.
>
> She was happy; her new dress had arrived.

Semi-colons are also used to separate complex lists, for example:

> Four men were in line for the prize: the previous winner; the young upstart; the old-stager; and the whizz-kid favourite.

Semi-colons are also used when a second clause adds information to the first clause, for example:

> I like coffee; my sister likes tea.

Colons

A colon (:) indicates a long pause in a sentence. It is a longer pause than the one created by a semi-colon, but not as long as the pause created by a full stop.

Colons can introduce lists, for example:

> The camera had many advantages: a viewfinder, dust removal, two free lenses and a flash.

Colons are also used before clauses which explain the first statement, for example:

> The manager was well respected: he looked after people, complimented them often and bought them presents when they did well.

Colons are sometimes used before a quotation or speech, for example:

> The King spoke: "Now is the time that we must all pull together."

Key words   semi-colon • colon • quotation

Semi-colons

1 Rewrite each of the following sentences so that it contains at least one semi-colon. You may need to replace other punctuation marks or even words.

a) Sarah is going home tomorrow and she will set out from there.

_____

b) We didn't finish the trip because it was too dark to stay out.

_____

c) I am going out now. I really need a break from my revision. I'll be home for tea.

_____

d) It rained heavily all day, but we still went for our walk. We needed the exercise!

_____

e) There were many different people taking part: the enthusiastic youngsters from the village, the veteran performers who won a number of awards, the local group and the weekend amateurs.

_____

_____

5

Colons

1 Put colons in the correct places in each of these sentences.

a) There were only two things that Fred worried about where the colon went and why it was used.

b) He only needed one thing to get through the week money.

c) Rule number one the teacher is always right.

d) Everything went right on that day they won the lottery, the electricity came back on, Jane got a new job and their pet dog was found.

e) The teacher walked in and opened her mouth to speak "Pens down and pay attention to what I am going to say."

2 Write three sentences of your own, each of which must include a colon.

a) _____

b) _____

c) _____

8

Punctuation 2

Apostrophes of omission

Apostrophes of omission are used to replace missing letters. Letters are often missed out when people are talking and words are shortened. For example, 'cannot' gets shortened to 'can't'. The apostrophe stands for the missing letters 'no' from 'cannot'.

would not = wouldn't	she has = she's	could have = could've	I have = I've
are not = aren't	he is = he's	they are = they're	you are = you're

But there are a few exceptions, for example:

will not = won't
o'clock = this stands for the old-fashioned saying, 'of the clock'.

Apostrophes of possession

Apostrophes of possession are used to show belonging – when one thing belongs to another.

Rule 1
If a word does not end in 's', add **apostrophe and s** (**'s**) to show possession. For example:

It was Dave's book. = The book belongs to Dave. 'Dave' does not end in s so add **'s**.
The children's clothes were dirty. = The clothes belong to the children. 'Children' does not end in s so add **'s**.

Rule 2
If a word does end in 's', just add an **apostrophe** (**'**) after the s to show possession. For example:

It was James' book. = The book belongs to James. 'James' ends in s, so just add **'** after the s.
The girls' team won. = The team belongs to the girls (plural). 'Girls' ends in s, so add **'** after the s.

When using Rule 2 and speaking, you might sometimes pronounce an extra 's' for words that end in 's'. Try saying 'St James' Park'. You probably say it like 'St James's Park'. It is not wrong to add the extra 's' in this example but you will probably find it easier to remember to add just an apostrophe when writing a word that ends in 's'.

It's and its

People often mix up the words 'it's' and 'its'. All you need to remember is:

It's = it is / it has, e.g. It's a long way from here. / It's been a nice day.
Its = belonging to it, e.g. The cat was washing its paws.

Key words   apostrophe of omission • apostrophe of possession

Apostrophes of omission

1 Put the apostrophes of omission into these sentences.

   a) Saffron couldnt believe that she had got the question wrong.

   b) Dean hadnt done his homework.

   c) Kayleigh shouldnt have eaten all the cakes.

   d) "Ive got it!" shouted Ryan.

   e) "Wheres the exit?" asked Ahmed.

   f) "I couldve done that!" remarked Rachel.

   g) "Lucy wont do the reading," explained Miss Sowter.

2 Change each of the following sets of words into one word by adding an apostrophe of omission.

   a) I had _____   **b)** You will _____

   c) They have _____   **d)** Do not _____   (11)

Apostrophes of possession

1 Put the apostrophes of possession in the correct places in these sentences.

   a) Joes pub is in New York.

   b) Nobody understood why Olivers answer was wrong.

   c) Lots of boys teams took part in the competition.

   d) Matthew was distracted by the womens chatter.

   e) James excuse for not doing his homework wasn't accepted by the teacher.

   f) Sairas bag had broken.

   g) The girls book was returned to her.

2 Are the apostrophes in the correct place in the following sentences?

	Correct	Incorrect
a) Jessie's hat was missing.	☐	☐
b) The womans' bag had been stolen.	☐	☐
c) Anil' had borrowed Jasons bike.	☐	☐

(10)

It's and its

1 Circle the correct option in the following sentences.

   a) **It's / Its** a nice day for a walk.

   b) The glass had lost **it's / its** shine.

(2)

Practise

Writing

Total marks (23)

11

Constructing paragraphs

Topics and paragraphs

A paragraph contains only one main topic. This is usually signalled by the opening sentence, which is called a topic sentence.

> <u>I believe that school uniform should be banned because of the cost to parents, who might have to buy a school uniform in addition to everyday clothes for their children.</u> Many poorer parents do not have sufficient money to spend on expensive uniforms, and while other clothes can be washed and re-used for a variety of situations, school uniform can only really be worn in one situation.

← *Topic sentence*

In a well-organised piece of writing, you can often get an overview of what it is about just by skimming and scanning the opening sentence of each paragraph. The topic at the start of the paragraph will then be developed as the paragraph goes on.

> I believe that school uniform should be banned because of the cost to parents, who might have to buy school uniform in addition to everyday clothes for their children. <u>Many poorer parents do not have sufficient money to spend on expensive uniforms, and while other clothes can be washed and re-used for a variety of situations, school uniform can only really be worn in one situation. Children nowadays like to have a sense of individuality and identity – and uniforms prevent this.</u>

← *Topic developed in the rest of the paragraph*

Paragraph length

There are no set rules on paragraph length. Paragraph length can be varied for effect.

Longer paragraphs might contain a detailed description of one person or scene. Shorter paragraphs might be used to shock or contrast, or to make a sudden point. Read the following example.

> The old sea captain sat up firmly against the harbour wall. His wizened face showed years of travel and damage from the merciless sun and the ocean winds. Thin lines ran out from his eyes like tiny rivers, and across his forehead great ravines scarred his skin where he had wrinkled his brow to keep out the spray from the North Atlantic gales. In his hands was an old pipe, from which little curls of smoke spasmodically ventured out and disappeared into nothingness.

← *Longer descriptive paragraph*

> He stood up. It was time to take to the seas again, one last time.

← *Shorter paragraph for impact*

💡 *Try using short paragraphs after long ones to create contrasts and for effect.*

Key words   topic sentence • contrast

Topics and paragraphs

1 Two topic sentences have been provided below. Complete the paragraphs, based on the topic sentences. Continue on a separate sheet of paper if necessary.

a) *I believe that school uniform is a good idea because everyone who wears it feels a sense of pride in their school.*

_____

_____

_____

_____

b) *The creature appeared out of the moon crater and came lumbering towards the astronauts.*

_____

_____

_____

_____

10

Paragraph length

1 Here is a short paragraph. Write a longer descriptive paragraph that might come **before** it. Continue on a separate sheet of paper if necessary.

She stopped. It was surely time for the bell to ring.

_____

_____

_____

_____

2 Here is another short paragraph. Write a longer factual paragraph that might come **before** it. Continue on a separate sheet of paper if necessary.

So, without doubt, you should spend your holiday in Rome. It's got everything!

_____

_____

_____

_____

10

Total marks 20

Linking paragraphs and sentences

Connectives

The first sentence of a paragraph is called the **topic sentence**. This highlights the main topic of the paragraph. After that, ideas need to be linked using a range of connectives, which will vary, depending on the style of writing.

Connectives are words / phrases that link paragraphs, or sentences within paragraphs. Different types of connective are used to link ideas in different ways. The table below shows some of the more typical connectives that can be used.

Connective	Description	Examples
Connectives of addition	Add extra information.	And, Also, Furthermore, Too, In addition, As well as, Again
Connectives of cause and effect	Show the effects of a previous idea / ideas.	Thus, So, Hence, As a result, Because, As, Therefore
Connectives of comparison	Look at similarities.	Equally, Compared to, Likewise, As with, Similarly
Connectives of contrast or balance	Show opposing ideas.	However, But, Alternatively, Yet, Although, On the other hand, Apart from, Nevertheless
Connectives of persuasion	Suggest that the reader will / should agree.	Of course, Certainly, Naturally, Obviously, Surely, Clearly, Evidently
Connectives of sequence / order / time	Show how ideas relate to each other in terms of their order.	Initially, At first, Firstly, Finally, Then, So far, Meanwhile, Eventually
Connectives of restriction	Show how ideas might be limited.	Only if, Unless, Save for, Except for
Connectives of emphasis	Help to highlight ideas.	Above all, In particular, Specifically, Importantly, Indeed, In fact, Notably
Connectives of illustration	Introduce examples.	For example, For instance, Such as, As shown by, As illustrated by
Connectives of summary	Introduce an overall view, conclusion or summary.	Overall, In brief, In all, To sum up, In summary, On the whole, In conclusion

Key words   connectives

Connectives

1 Read the paragraph below, which includes five connectives. Write each of the five connectives in the table below and state what type of connective each one is.

Firstly, I would like to announce that I will be standing for the school council. So far, I have served the school in a number of ways. I have been a tutor group representative, library helper and Sports leader for my year. Consequently, I feel that I am in a strong position to stand for the vacant post on the council; in brief – I am the best candidate!

Connective	Type of connective
a)	
b)	
c)	
d)	
e)	

2 Write your own paragraph, using the following connectives only once and in any order you like. Continue on a separate sheet of paper if necessary.

        thus   **finally**   **but**   **clearly**

_____

_____

_____

_____

_____

3 In the paragraph below, circle the most suitable connective from the choices given to make the whole paragraph make sense.

Initially / Secondly / Subsequently, I would like to explain why I am here. **On the other hand / In addition to / Finally** my appearance at last night's awards ceremony, I wanted to express my thanks at greater length than I was able to yesterday. **Nevertheless / In particular / Otherwise**, I would like to say thank you to my English teacher, who inspired me to write songs. **Throughout / Equally / Apart from** his support, I received no encouragement at all in my teenage years.

13

Total marks 13

Connectives and signposts

Connectives as transitions

Connectives sometimes form part of a set of words to show a move from one completed thought to another. When a connective does this, it is part of a transition. Transitions show what idea has come first and what follows. Look at these examples:

- **In addition to** winning the European music award, the teacher **also** took part in the school show.
- **So much for** the winner; **what about** the loser?
- **As we know** so little about Anglo-Saxon times, **let us turn** to the new archaeological discoveries to help us.

In each of the examples above, the connectives are made of two separated parts that form a transition. The transition links the different ideas together.

Connectives as signposts

Signposts are short statements or words that provide a clue about where the writer is in their speech, argument, etc. Sometimes, signposts can give the reader clues to the importance of the words that will follow. Look at these examples:

- Let us **first** take notice of the main issue under discussion.
- The **third** problem is losing the ability to focus properly.
- The **last**, and **most important thing** to remember is that you should look after your camera.
- **To conclude**, we should consider what we have just discussed.

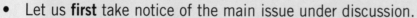

In each of the examples above, the signpost indicates what will follow. For example, the signpost 'last' tells the reader that this is the final point and the signpost 'to conclude' tells the reader that the writing is being concluded.

 Do not use number signposts (e.g. 'First', 'Second', 'Third') too repetitively. They could make your writing become boring.

Combining connectives and signposts

By combining connectives, creating transitions and using signposts, you will give your writing structure and enable it to flow. Look at this example:

Firstly, and most importantly, little is known about Viking times, **so** we need to read more. After reading more, we may find out more, **but** the chances of this happening are slim, **because** there is not enough written down to help us.

Red = Signposts   Blue = Connectives

Key words   transition • signpost

Connectives as transitions

1 Underline the connectives and / or transitions in these sentences.

Example: <u>As</u> we know who won, <u>let us</u> forget the result.

a) So much for the school work; what about the holidays?

b) Since we know a great deal about football, let us turn to the subject of hockey.

c) Although they won the lottery, they also continued to work.

d) Despite eating too much, they still enjoyed the meal.

2 Write your own sentences, using the two transition parts provided.

Example: In addition to / finally: In addition to seeing the gig, they finally got to meet their hero.

a) In addition to / furthermore _____

b) Besides / also _____

c) In spite of / although _____

d) Despite / on the other hand _____

8

Connectives as signposts

1 Underline the signposts in each of these sentences.

a) Let's first take a look at what happened.

b) The second problem relates to the views of the government.

c) To begin with, we must review what we know.

d) To conclude, we should consider all the evidence.

e) Initially – and most importantly – there is the matter of who will pay.

5

Combining connectives and signposts

1 Write a short paragraph about your favourite holiday. Make sure you use connectives, transitions and signposts. Continue on a separate sheet of paper if necessary.

_____

_____

_____

_____

5

Total marks 18

Voice

Writing in a consistent voice

You need to be able to write in a consistent **voice**. Voice is what a reader hears when they read a piece of writing. The voice that you use in your writing will depend on:
- The purpose – why you are writing.
- The audience – who you are writing for.

A consistent voice is one which meets the following criteria:
- Viewpoint will be consistent.
- Style will be appropriate throughout – it should be formal or informal.
- Tenses will be consistent and appropriate throughout – it should use the **past tense** (e.g. I went), the **present tense** (e.g. I go / I am going), or the **future tense** (I will go).
- Vocabulary will be consistent and appropriate throughout.
- Sentences will be controlled and appropriate.

But voice can also vary, just as a person's voice might change when speaking. As long as it sounds appropriate throughout, it is regarded as consistent.

Look at this example of a formal text:

> In order for **us** to understand what **is** meant by a **consistent** voice in writing, **we** need to learn from the writing of others. **It is** also useful for **us** to learn from **our** own mistakes and the mistakes of others. By doing this, **we**, as writers, can achieve at least a Level 6 standard when **judged** against the **National Curriculum standards**. If writing **formally**, then **formality needs** to be **maintained**, so that the **tone** of the writing **is appropriate** throughout.
>
> Purple = consistent viewpoint   Blue = controlled tenses   Green = consistent level and type of vocabulary

The overall effect is one of control and the same voice talking throughout. This is not only seen in formal writing, though; it can be just as evident in creative or informal writing.

Look at this informal piece of speech that you might find in a story for teenagers:

> "What do **you mean**? **You're** right **dozy, you** are! **I can't believe you've** gone and **messed** up all **me** good work. **I spent** ages doing that up and now it's **a total mess**. All **me** dreams **are** shattered – how **am** I **gonna** win the competition now?"
>
> Purple = consistent viewpoint
>
> Blue = controlled tenses
>
> Green = consistent level and type of vocabulary

Both examples on this page show that it is possible to control your writing and create a consistent voice, regardless of the purpose and audience of the writing.

Key words   purpose • audience • tense • vocabulary

Writing in a consistent voice

1 Read the passage below. It does not have a consistent voice because the tenses are inconsistent.

Emily is going to school and caught the bus. She ran from the bus-park and enters the school through its main gates. After doing this she is worn out because she had run out of breath. Her teacher is waiting and told her off for coming into the classroom with messy uniform.

a) Re-write the passage in the past tense to create a consistent voice.

_____

_____

_____

_____

_____

b) Now write the next paragraph, continuing in the past tense.

_____

_____

_____

_____

2 Read the passage below. In each case, circle the most appropriate word from the three options, in order to create a formal tone.

The main reason why the Anglo-Saxons **nicked / stuffed / buried** treasure was, we believe, to keep it safe from raiders. **Brain-boxes / Experts / Clever-clogs** are still debating the significance of the treasure **swag / hoard / boodle** found in Staffordshire, but it may never reveal its secrets. One expert was **rumoured / parroted / quoted** as saying that recent discoveries have made us change completely the way that we view the **ancient / past-it / decrepit** world and that many of our history books will need to be re-written.

3 Complete the passage below. The writer's intention is to create a spooky, mysterious atmosphere, so the words that you place in the gaps should all help to create that mood. Do not repeat a word, even if it is a good one.

Bill walked _____ to the _____ door. The

_____ house in front of him made him feel _____ . Little

did he know what _____ things lay inside, lurking in the

_____ shadows, waiting for someone like him to arrive. He

_____ pushed the door open and stepped inside. From the

darkness he heard the _____ sound of _____ .

24

Practise

Writing

Total marks   24

19

Adding originality 1

At Level 6, you should be adding originality into your writing. There are several tips and tricks to help you do this.

Adjectives

Adjectives describe nouns. They add extra detail to writing. Sometimes, it helps to build up mood in your writing if you add extra adjectives at key points. Instead of one adjective, why not use two – or even three? Look at the difference it can make:

The man walked into the room. ⟶ The man walked into the **dull**, **oppressive** room.

The second sentence is more effective because it builds up a stronger picture in the reader's mind of what the room is like.

Be careful that you do not overdo the adjectives though. If you use two or three adjectives every time a description is needed, your writing will become repetitive and difficult to read. Only double or triple the adjectives in places where you want to have a really powerful effect.

Alliteration

You could choose words that begin with the same letter or the same sound. This is called alliteration and this can add even more emphasis. For example:

The girl ate the sweets. ⟶ The girl ate the **sickly**, **sticky** sweets.
She threw away the flowers. ⟶ She threw away the **limp**, **lifeless** flowers.

The second sentences are more effective because they provide more detail and add emphasis.

Similes

A simile is a form of imagery. A simile always contains the word 'as' or 'like', for example:
- His hands were as cold as ice.
- He grunted like a pig when he walked past us.

Using similes is a good way to add description but make sure they are original. Some similes are overused and clichéd. But, you could start with a common simile and alter it by adding extra detail of your own. For example, you might wish to add an extra adjective or an extra clause:

The child was as quiet as a mouse. ⟶ The child was as quiet as a **terrified** mouse.
The child was as quiet as a terrified mouse. ⟶ The child was as quiet as a terrified mouse, **about to be pounced on by a cat.**

Take care not to over-exaggerate when adding extra adjectives or clauses to a simile.

Key words   adjective • noun • alliteration • simile • imagery

Adjectives

1 Improve these sentences by adding two extra adjectives in the gaps. There are several possible adjectives you could use.

a) Laura hid her _____ photos from her friends.

b) Mia's _____ dress was an absolute sensation.

c) No-one took any notice of Rob's _____ mood.

d) The _____ computer let Tom down.

e) Olivia's _____ brother really irritated her.

f) Wade's _____ shirt cost a fortune.

6

Alliteration

1 Improve these sentences by placing two adjectives in the gap to create alliteration.

a) The _____ snake slithered into the garden.

b) The _____ trees swayed in the breeze.

c) The house was _____ and _____ .

d) She put the _____ ring on her finger.

e) It was a _____ smell that wafted through the house.

5

Similes

1 Make these clichéd similes original by placing one or two adjectives in the gap.

a) As playful as a _____ kitten.

b) As clean as a _____ whistle.

c) As clear as _____ mud.

d) As dull as _____ dishwater.

e) As stubborn as a _____ mule.

2 Make these clichéd similes original by placing an extra clause after them.

a) He was as poor as a church mouse _____

b) Her hands were as cold as ice _____

c) The cake was as flat as a pancake _____

d) Her daughter is as white as a ghost _____

e) That man is as cool as a cucumber _____

10

Total marks **21**

Adding originality 2

Avoiding clichés and common mistakes

To make sure that your writing is original and of a high quality, you should avoid using clichés and making common mistakes.

For example:

- When writing a story, do not end it with, 'and then I woke up and it was all a dream.'.
- Do not give unnecessary lists, especially of people's names, e.g. 'I went to the shops with Baz, Daz, Kaz and Wazzer.'.
- Try not to use common, overused similes, e.g. 'as sick as a parrot'.
- Avoid repeating the same words several times in one piece of writing.
- Try to use a variety of sentence types.
- Avoid mixed metaphors, e.g. 'If we can hit that bullseye, then the rest of the cards will fall like a set of dominoes'.
- Do not write too much if it is not needed. It is better to have a short, high quality piece of writing than a long, repetitive piece of writing.
- Do not use 'big' words to try to make yourself sound clever if you do not fully understand them or know how to use them; you will just end up highlighting a lack of knowledge.
- Make sure that you are consistent in your use of tenses. It can confuse the reader if you switch from past tense to present tense – or vice-versa – without good reason.

Planning and drafting

You will find it helpful to plan your writing before you begin. Planning means you will place your best ideas in the most appropriate places in your writing.

No matter what style of writing you are engaged in, the opening, the key moments in the middle and the ending are very important:

- **The opening** needs to have impact. Ask yourself: What kind of impact? How am I going to grab the reader's attention? What is the purpose of my writing? How am I going to achieve it?
- **The key moments** are the main sections of your writing. Ask yourself: Which sections do I want to have the biggest impact on the reader? Why? How am I going to achieve that impact?
- **The ending** needs to be clear and should tie in all the key moments of the writing. Ask yourself: What do I want to leave the reader thinking, feeling or knowing? How am I going to achieve that?

By considering these questions, your writing will appear more structured and more original. By thinking about what techniques to use and where to put them, your writing will have greater impact and force on the reader.

Key words   cliché • metaphor

Avoiding clichés and common mistakes

1 Complete your own paragraph plan for the following task: 'Write a short description of a place that has had a big effect on you.' Write a summary of what each paragraph will be about in the 'Paragraph plan' column. Then write down what descriptive techniques you might use in the 'Techniques to use' column. Continue on a separate sheet of paper if necessary.

Paragraph plan	Techniques to use

12

Planning and drafting

1 Below is a paragraph plan for a persuasive speech and a list of techniques to use. Match the plan with the techniques by putting the appropriate letter in the correct box.

1. State the purpose of the speech. ☐

2. First point – an important one. ☐

3. Second point – uses the opposing view to back up own argument. ☐

4. Most important point. ☐

5. Final summary. ☐

A Use a rhetorical question to grab attention.
B Use persuasive rule of three to sum up and add impact.
C Use exaggeration for emphasis.
D Use flattery to get the audience on your side.
E Use connectives of opposition to bring in opposing ideas.

5

Total marks 17

Adverbs

What are adverbs?

Adverbs are used to describe how something happens. They describe **verbs**, such as 'run', 'sing', 'chase', 'goes'. Many – but not all – adverbs end in 'ly', for example, 'quickly', 'happily', 'fiercely'. But you can only really tell an adverb from the job it does in a sentence.

Some words ending in 'ly' are not adverbs. These include 'lovely', 'lonely' and 'friendly', which are adjectives because they describe nouns, e.g. 'A friendly person'.

Some common words that do not end in 'ly' can be used as adverbs. These include:

- 'almost', e.g. She almost cried.
- 'too', e.g. My parents ate too.
- 'more', e.g. He sang more than his sister.
- 'never', e.g. Mohammed never helped.
- 'far', e.g. The cat ran far.

- 'less', e.g. I couldn't care less.
- 'always', e.g. He always ran.
- 'even', e.g. Ben even danced.
- 'well', e.g. They played well.
- 'often', e.g. Charlie often had a headache.

Some words can act as both adjectives and adverbs:

Word	As an adjective	As an adverb
fast	He drove a fast car.	She drove fast.
high	It was a very high building.	The bird flew high.
low	She got a low score.	He kept low to the floor.
late	She had a late night.	She arrived late.

Positioning adverbs

Adverbs can be put in different places in sentences to achieve different effects.

By placing an adverb **before** the verb, you can emphasise the 'how' part of the action. For example:
- Todd *quickly* ran to the exit.

Here, 'quickly' comes first, so it has greater emphasis in the sentence than the verb 'ran'. But not all adverbs fit comfortably before the verb.

By placing an adverb **after** the verb, you place greater emphasis on the verb itself. For example:
- Todd ran to the exit *quickly*.

If you place the adverb at the start of the sentence, you create tension because it takes longer for the reader to get to the verb (which tells you what is happening in the sentence). Note that if you start a sentence with an adverb, it needs a comma after it. For example:
- *Quickly*, Todd ran to the exit.

Use adverbs to add subtle emphasis to different parts of your sentences. Try placing them in different parts of sentences and read the sentences out loud to get a feel for where they fit best.

Key words   adverb • verb

What are adverbs?

1 <u>Underline</u> the adverb in each of these sentences.

a) Annoyingly, Richard was right.

b) Tom fortunately got the message in the nick of time.

c) Ed almost won the lottery.

d) Sandra got her homework done hurriedly.

e) Someone always loses.

f) Surprisingly, Shauna sat next to one of the boys.

g) Fiona ate her dinner lazily.

2 Circle the best adverb from the choices given, to complete these sentences.

a) Chrissy **quickly / stupidly / remorselessly** ate her dinner so that she didn't miss the bus.

b) **Easily / Lazily / Cleverly**, Joey got out of bed in the middle of the afternoon.

c) Johnny played his guitar **domestically / principally / accurately**.

d) Tommy **desperately / romantically / carefully** cuts sandwiches with a sharp knife.

e) Dee Dee, when angry, complains **dreamily / sensitively / loudly**.

f) Richie plays tennis **aggressively / swimmingly / thoughtlessly**.

g) Mark **verifiably / honestly / enthusiastically** took part in the football match.

14

Positioning adverbs

1 Rewrite each of the following sentences, putting the adverb(s) in a different position.

a) Syed was wrong fortunately.

_____

b) Tara carelessly gave away the answer by speaking loudly.

_____

c) Bob wrote a great article for the paper but stupidly lost it.

_____

d) Daniel excitedly published his pictures.

_____

e) Francis easily wins the egg-and-spoon race and cheers triumphantly afterwards.

_____

5

Total marks 19

Vocabulary 1

Using a thesaurus

At Level 6 you will need to use less commonly used words. One of the best ways to do this is to use a **thesaurus**. But you need to be careful when using a thesaurus, because you need to pick a word with an appropriate shade of meaning or **context** for what you want to say.

Example

Jimmy wanted to use a better word than 'big' to describe a soldier in a story he was writing. His sentence was this: 'The big soldier charged angrily towards me.'

Jimmy looked up 'big' in the thesaurus and this is what he found:

> ample, awash, brimming, bulky, burly, capacious, chock-full, colossal, commodious, considerable, copious, crowded, enormous, extensive, fat, full, gigantic, heavy-duty, heavyweight, hefty, huge, hulking, humongous, husky, immense, jumbo, mammoth, massive, mondo, monster, oversize, packed, ponderous, prodigious, roomy, sizable, spacious, strapping, stuffed, substantial, super colossal, thundering, tremendous, vast, voluminous, whopping.

There are plenty of options here, but not all of them would fit in the sentence that Jimmy is trying to write. Jimmy reduced the list by taking out all the words that he knew definitely could not be used in his sentence.

Jimmy also wanted to improve his **vocabulary**, so he reduced the list further by taking out some of the more commonly used words in the list. This left him with the following:

> ample, bulky, burly, colossal, considerable, copious, enormous, heavyweight, hefty, hulking, humongous, immense, jumbo, mammoth, monster, strapping, super colossal, thundering, tremendous, whopping.

Jimmy also then used a dictionary to find the right shade of meaning for the words. His favourites were:

* Hulking – meaning heavy and clumsy.
* Burly – meaning large in bodily size; sturdy or stout.
* Hefty – meaning big, strong, powerful and muscular.

Jimmy chose 'hefty' because the word contained a feeling of power that he wanted to create in his description. So his sentence became: 'The hefty soldier charged angrily towards me.'

If you can avoid using common words and instead replace them with more interesting words, your work will be more original, more interesting and of a higher quality. As well as adjectives like 'hefty', try to use more interesting nouns, verbs and adverbs too. For example:

* House ⟶ Mansion, Cottage, Bungalow
* Walk ⟶ Saunter, Stroll, Amble
* Quickly ⟶ Rapidly, Swiftly, Hastily

Always use a dictionary with a thesaurus so that you know you are choosing a word that has the correct shade of meaning for your writing.

Key words   thesaurus • context • vocabulary

Using a thesaurus

1 Use a thesaurus to find a less common replacement word for the underlined word in each of the following sentences.

a) Mike was a <u>terrible</u> footballer. _____

b) The hills were <u>big</u>. _____

c) Silvana sang <u>well</u>. _____

d) Gareth felt <u>bad</u>. _____

e) The house was <u>old</u>. _____

f) The bully got involved in a <u>fight</u>. _____

g) The weather was <u>cold</u>. _____

h) Dave's camera was <u>good</u>. _____

i) Rachel bought a(n) <u>expensive</u> dress. _____

2 For each of the commonly used words in the table below, circle the word that is closest to it in meaning from the options given in the less commonly used word list.

Commonly used word	Less commonly used word
a) Rough	**Brambly / Tough / Capacious**
b) Lazy	**Abnormal / Apathetic / Audacious**
c) Smelly	**Magnanimous / Malodorous / Munificent**
d) Beautiful	**Exquisite / Abhorrent / Jovial**
e) Big	**Vacuous / Voluminous / Erudite**
f) Small	**Doddering / Diminutive / Crude**
g) Old	**Diffident / Germinated / Geriatric**
h) Young	**Arid / Adolescent / Pneumatic**
i) Smooth	**Lustrous / Asinine / Tumultuous**

3 Here are some less commonly used words. Use each one correctly in a sentence. Use a dictionary to find their meanings if you do not know them.

a) Ineffable _____

b) Ludicrous _____

c) Pertinent _____

d) Supremacy _____

e) Ridicule _____

23

Total marks 23

Vocabulary 2

Expanding your vocabulary

The problem with trying to prepare to demonstrate Level 6 vocabulary under controlled conditions in an examination, is that you do not know what the topic will be, so it is difficult to learn banks of words, as they may be irrelevant to the topic that you are given.

But it is worth trying to expand your vocabulary as much as you can. If you can learn some words that you could use in a variety of situations, they will be helpful to you in an exam.

Try to learn a selection of words that have general meanings and that you are likely to use in any type of writing. For example, learn a variety of synonyms for 'good', 'bad', etc.

'Good' words

In most kinds of writing, you will need to use words that show some sort of positive opinion. There are lots of words that are not so commonly used, which mean 'good' in some way, and which can be applied to a variety of situations.

> **Word bank of 'good' words**
> acceptable, admirable, agreeable, choice, commendable, congenial, deluxe, exceptional, favourable, first-class, first-rate, gratifying, honourable, marvellous, positive, prime, reputable, satisfactory, satisfying, select, shipshape, splendid, sterling, stupendous, super-eminent, excellent, superior, tip-top, valuable, welcome, wonderful, worthy, blameless, charitable, dutiful, ethical, exemplary, guiltless, honest, honourable, incorrupt, inculpable, irreprehensible, irreproachable, obedient, praiseworthy, pure, reputable, respectable, righteous, tractable, uncorrupted, untainted, upright, valuable, well-behaved.

'Bad' words

Equally, in most kinds of writing, you will need to use words that show some sort of negative opinion.

> **Word bank of 'bad' words**
> abominable, amiss, atrocious, beastly, bottom out, bummer, careless, cruddy, crummy, defective, deficient, diddly, dissatisfactory, fallacious, garbage, gross, grungy, imperfect, inadequate, incorrect, inferior, junky, lousy, slipshod, stinking, substandard, synthetic, unacceptable, unsatisfactory.

Make sure that you use a dictionary to find out the exact shade of meaning of 'good' or 'bad' that the words in these word banks convey.

Key words   synonym

'Good' words

❶ Complete these sentences by choosing an appropriate 'good' word from the word bank on the facing page. Try to use a different word in each sentence.

a) The football match was most _____ .

b) Zafar strolled into the _____ hotel.

c) Tara's concern was _____ .

d) The politician was completely _____ .

e) The _____ film amazed the viewers.

f) _____ flowers filled the garden in the spring-time.

g) The boy's guitar playing was _____ .

h) It could be argued that banning school uniform is a really _____ idea.

i) Old songs are usually _____ .

j) The _____ gesture made their day.

10

'Bad' words

❶ Complete these sentences by choosing an appropriate 'bad' word from the word bank on the facing page. Try to use a different word in each sentence.

a) The team's performance was _____ .

b) Failing to reach your target grade is _____ .

c) The surfer thought that the lack of waves was a _____ .

d) Debbie disliked the _____ excuses she had heard.

e) _____ ideas don't help.

f) _____ sentences won't earn you many marks.

g) The _____ house didn't please the prospective buyers.

h) The girl's _____ story didn't convince the teacher.

i) _____ goods are often bought off the internet.

j) The _____ car broke down.

10

Practise | Writing

Spelling 1

Writing

Learn

Spelling rules

There are several ways to learn tricky spellings. You could try creating a **spelling log** in which you make a list of words that you find difficult to spell. Every time you use a new word, check it in a dictionary. Make sure you understand what it means and that you know how to spell it.

It will also help you to keep spelling rules in your spelling log. Here are some common spelling rules you might wish to learn:
- 'q' is always followed with 'u': 'qu'.
- 'i' comes before 'e' when it is pronounced as 'ee', except when it follows the letter 'c'
- 'e' comes before 'i' when sounded like ('ay') as in neighbour and weigh.
- 'i' and 'e' are sometimes used together and sounded as separate vowels, e.g. in diet, quiet.
- 'ti', 'ci', 'si' are three pairs of letters used to produce a 'sh' sound. So remember that not all words with a 'sh' sound are spelt with 'sh'. For example, station, suspicion, intermission.
- If you add a suffix to a word ending in -e:
  - Keep the -e if the suffix begins with a consonant, e.g. grace ⟶ graceful
  - Drop the -e if the suffix begins with a vowel, e.g. save ⟶ saving
- In a two-syllable word, it is usual for a short vowel to take a double consonant after it, and a long vowel to take a single consonant after it, e.g.
  - Short vowel: latter, bitter, dinner, holly.
  - Long vowel: later, biter, diner, holy.

*Invent mnemonics for words that you have trouble remembering how to spell, e.g. **N**ot **E**very **C**at **E**ats **S**quidgy **S**ausages **A**nd **R**hubarb **Y**oghurt. The initial letters spell the word 'necessary'.*

Syllables and phonemes

A **syllable** is a part of a word that contains a vowel sound. Breaking down longer words into syllables makes it easier to spell them. For example:
- educational ⟶ ed–u–ca–tion–al (5 syllables)

A phoneme is an individual sound in a word. Breaking down longer words into phonemes can help you to spell them correctly because you are less likely to miss letters out. For example:
- paint ⟶ p–ai–n–t (4 phonemes, 1 syllable)

ph - o - n - e - me

Root words

A root word is a word that can have an extra part attached to the beginning (a prefix) or the end (a **suffix**). For example, 'inter' is a root word, which can form the words 'international', 'internal' and 'interview' by adding suffixes.

Key words   vowel • suffix • consonant • syllable • mnemonic • phoneme • prefix

Spelling rules

1 In these sentences, there is a gap where either 'ie' or 'ei' should go. Fill in the correct letters.

    a) 'I would like a p _____ ce of that cake.'

    b) Make sure that you only write a br_____ f answer.

    c) W_____ gh vegetables before cooking.

2 Underline the correct spelling from each choice of two in these sentences.

    a) I will see you **latter** / **later**.

    b) The **latter** / **later** describes the most up-to-date procedures.

    c) The jealous man felt really **biter** / **bitter**.

    d) The dog was known as a **biter** / **bitter**.

3 Underline the correct spelling in each group of three.

    a) **Rasspberry** / **Raspberry** / **Razberry**   **b)** **Februay** / **Februery** / **February**

    c) **Necessity** / **Neccessity** / **Neccessaty**   **d)** **Libary** / **Librery** / **Library**

    e) **Naybor** / **Neighbour** / **Nieghbour**   **f)** **Hypocrissy** / **Hypocrisy** / **Hypocrasy**

    g) **Adrress** / **Address** / **Adress**   **h)** **Dissappoint** / **Disappoint** / **Disapoint**

    i) **Busness** / **Business** / **Buisness**   **j)** **Rumour** / **Rumer** / **Roomor**

17

Syllables and phonemes

1 Write down how many syllables and phonemes are in each of these words.

Word	Number of syllables	Number of phonemes
a) politician		
b) computer		
c) pain		

6

Root words

1 What is the root of each of the following words? There is a clue for each one to help you. You are looking for the part that links to the clue.

Word	Clue	Root
a) pedal	'foot'	
b) biology	'life'	
c) chronology	'time'	

3

Total marks   26

Spelling 2

Writing

Learn

Adding suffixes

A suffix is a part of a word that can be added to an existing word to change its meaning. It may alter the **tense** (e.g. I walk ——→ I walked) or the **class** (e.g. employ (verb) ——→ employee (noun)). Here are some rules to help you with spelling when adding a suffix:

- For words ending in a single -l after a single vowel, double the 'l' before adding a suffix. For example:
  - travel ——→ trave**ll**ed
  - signal ——→ signa**ll**ed

  This rule also applies to words ending in a single -p, -d or -r for example:
  - wrap ——→ wra**pp**ed
  - mud ——→ mu**dd**y
  - occur ——→ occu**rr**ence
- For words that end in a single vowel and -t, and have the **stress** on the last syllable, double the final -t before adding a suffix. For example:
  - permit ——→ permi**tt**ed
  - admit ——→ admi**tt**ed
  - regret ——→ regre**tt**ed

  But not all words ending in a single vowel and -t double the -t when adding a suffix, e.g. visit ——→ visi**t**ed; benefit ——→ benefi**t**ed. This is because the stress is on the first syllable of the root or base word.

Forming plurals

Many words simply need the addition of -s to make them **plural**, e.g. animal ——→ animals; table ——→ tables. But some words need different spellings to make them plural.

Here are some general rules for forming plurals:
- To form plurals of words ending in -s, -ss, -x, -z, -sh, or -ch, add **-es**. For example, bu**ses**, gla**sses**, fo**xes**, buz**zes**, wi**shes**, chur**ches**.
- To form plurals of words ending in the consonant -y, you often need to change -y to **-ies**. For example, bab**ies**, strawberr**ies**. But be careful! Not all words ending in -y become -ies in the plural. If a word ends in a vowel then -y, just add -s, for example: toy ——→ toys.
- Most words that end in the letter 'f' become plural by adding the suffix -ves. For example:
  - shelf ——→ shel**ves**, wolf ——→ wol**ves**

  But note that there are a few words that do not fit this rule, for example:
  - chief ——→ chief**s**, roof ——→ roof**s**

There are a number of irregular plurals which do not fit any of these rules, for example: child ——→ children; coffee ——→ coffee; formula ——→ formulae. You need to just learn these as you come across them.

Key words   class • stress • plural

Adding suffixes

1 Add the correct suffix to each of the underlined words so that the sentences make sense.

> **Example**
> I <u>travel</u> to Egypt last year. ➡ I **travelled** to Egypt last year.

a) The food was <u>appal</u> _____

b) I <u>haul</u> _____ the bag onto my shoulders.

c) Caroline decided to dress <u>formal</u> _____ for the ball.

d) I <u>usual</u> _____ shop here.

e) "Do you live <u>local</u> _____ ?"

f) "Did you hear about the man who got <u>kidnap</u> _____ ?"

g) The incident <u>occur</u> _____ last Monday.

2 Add the correct suffix to each of the underlined words so that the sentences make sense.

> **Example**
> I was not <u>permit</u> to play football. ➡ I was not **permitted** to play football.

a) I <u>admit</u> _____ my guilt to the court yesterday.

b) Sheila <u>regret</u> _____ her actions.

c) I <u>benefit</u> _____ from last week's exercise.

d) I <u>visit</u> _____ my relations last month.

e) I have <u>commit</u> _____ no crime.

f) I was <u>visit</u> _____ my grandma when I heard.

g) I was <u>regret</u> _____ my decision already.

 14

Forming plurals

1 Write down the correct plural form for each of the following words.

a) Writer _____   **b)** Potato _____

c) Cherry _____   **d)** Monkey _____

e) Beach _____   **f)** Brother-in-law _____

g) Loaf _____   **h)** Mouse _____

i) Reef _____   **j)** Woman _____

k) Elephant _____   **l)** Rice _____

m) Cactus _____   **n)** Intelligence _____

o) Half _____   15

Total marks ⬤ 29

33

Organising your ideas

Planning

Before you do any kind of writing, you need to organise your ideas. You can do this in a variety of ways; different ways suit different people with different learning styles. It might help you to try out these different forms of planning to find out which one works best for you.

Planning in your mind

Advantages	Disadvantages
• It is quick and easy. • It is good for short responses where you do not have to write much and the writing only needs to be organised in a simple, straightforward way.	• It is no good for longer, or more complicated pieces of extended writing. It is too easy to forget things and get confused. • It is not easy (especially in exams when you are writing to a time limit) to keep the plan in your head and remember what needs to go in each part.

Making lists

Advantages	Disadvantages
• It is a simple and straightforward process. • It will help you to put ideas into a logical order. • Lists can easily be numbered to help with the sequence of your ideas.	• If you are aiming for high grades or levels, you will be expected to make cross-references and synthesise your ideas. Making lists might restrict how well you do this, stopping you from achieving the highest levels or grades.

Spider diagrams / mind maps

Advantages	Disadvantages
• They are good for generating ideas and for working at speed. • They are very good for organising the sequence and development of ideas.	• They can get messy and difficult to read if they contain a lot of information. They need to be numbered if they are going to be used to sequence your ideas. • They need space to be developed well.

💡 *You do not have to use the same planning method all the time. You can use different methods for different tasks. For example, in writing a story, you might brainstorm, but for an argumentative essay, you might make lists of points for and against the issue being discussed.*

Key words cross-reference

Planning

1 To discover which planning approach suits you best, plan an answer to the task below, using each of the three planning types. When you have done this, consider all three of your plans and see if you can work out which one has produced the best plan from which to write up an answer. (You do not have to write up the answer unless you want to!)

Task: 'Write a description of a place that has had a big effect on you.'

a) Planning in your mind	b) Making lists

c) Spider diagrams / mind maps

3

Total marks   3

Formal writing

Types of formal writing

There are many types of formal writing. Some of the more common types that you might come across include the following:

- Business letters
- Instructions
- Job applications
- Reports
- Educational books and reference books
- Letters of complaint

Formal writing can be produced for a variety of purposes, but all formal writing must have the following features:

- The writing needs to be clear.
- It needs to be as literal as possible.
- It needs to be well-structured and organised.
- It needs vocabulary that is suitable for its audience. It can be written from a variety of viewpoints, but the passive voice is often a good choice, because it makes the writing less personal and less biased, and therefore more formal.

If you look at the types of formal writing in the list above, you will see that in all cases you will want to create a good impression on the person reading. For example, in business letters and job applications, your aim would be to acquire a contract or a job; in educational writing, you would want your ideas to come across as clear and well-structured so that you can gain credit in exams or in controlled assessment; if you were a teacher writing a report, you would have to write very formally so that the report did not come across as too personal and biased.

Formal letters

Letters are one of the more common types of formal writing. The rules for writing letters have changed over time and will continue to change, meaning that there are no definite right or wrong rules – only generally accepted ones. For example, some companies have a house style of putting the sender's and the receiver's addresses on the same side; others will have them on opposing sides.

Some of the more common features of formal letters are listed below, but you may find slight variations on these in practice.

- There should be an address to which you are writing and your return address should be included too.
- There should be a date indicating when you wrote the letter.
- There needs to be an appropriately formal greeting, e.g. Dear Sir, Dear Madam, Dear Mr. Jones.
- There needs to be an appropriately formal ending, e.g. Yours faithfully (if you don't know the name of the person you have written to); Your sincerely (if you have named the person you are writing to in your opening greeting).

When writing a formal letter, put yourself in the position of the person receiving it – what would they think of your letter?

Key words   formal • passive voice • biased

Answers

PAGE 5

Sentence parts

1. a) (Becky didn't do her homework), because she had lost her book.
    b) (Sadie said that she understood the work), even though it was difficult.
    c) Despite being well behaved, (Alex was told off by the teacher.)
    d) Although she had been away, (Laura got top marks in the exam.)
    e) (Sara laughed), because Sophie dropped her sweets.
    f) (Emily's work was good) despite being untidy.
    g) Because she had a cold, (Courtney was absent.)

2. a) Because she had lost her book, Becky didn't do her homework.
    b) Even though it was difficult, Sadie said that she understood the work.
    c) Alex was told off by the teacher, despite being well behaved.
    d) Laura got top marks in the exam, although she had been away.
    e) Because Sophie dropped her sweets, Sara laughed.
    f) Despite being untidy, Emily's work was good.
    g) Courtney was absent, because she had a cold.

Sentences with more than two clauses

1. a) Although he was very young, Grant was a great musician, who many admired.
    b) Mike loved painting, because it gave him an extra income, alongside his teaching job.
    c) Although his children didn't like it, Gerald's beard grew, because he didn't shave.

2. **Here are some possible rearrangements – there are other possible answers:**
    a) Grant was a great musician, who many admired, although he was very young.
    b) Mike loved painting, alongside his teaching job, because it gave him an extra income.
    c) Gerald's beard grew, although his children didn't like it, because he didn't shave.

PAGE 7

Short sentences

1. **There are many possible answers, e.g.**
    a) It suddenly shot up. b) 'Don't leave!'
    c) I was right. d) The door slammed. e) Go home.
    f) The water freezes into ice. The ice expands.

Long sentences

1. **There are many possible answers, e.g.**
    a) The velvety black cat gradually unravelled itself from its long sleep and stood up and stretched, its sharp claws digging into the hard wooden floor.
    b) When the water reaches freezing point, it turns into ice, expanding and causing the rock to crack and become weaker.
    c) The mysterious shape cast a long, dark shadow across the corridor – a shadow that moved slowly but surely, getting closer to where we were standing, frightened and trembling.
    d) I always knew that my answer was the correct one, just by the fact that the others had come up with an entirely different answer.
    e) If she hadn't worked so hard and been so diligent at school, she wouldn't have been able to go to university, where she gained her degree and became a successful businesswoman.

PAGE 9

Semi-colons

1. a) Sarah is going home tomorrow; she will set out from there.
    b) We didn't finish the trip; it was too dark to stay out.
    c) I am going out now; I really need a break from my revision. I'll be home for tea.
    d) It rained heavily all day, but we still went for our walk; we needed the exercise!
    e) There were many different people taking part: the enthusiastic youngsters from the village; the veteran performers who won a number of awards; the local group; and the weekend amateurs.

© Letts Educational Ltd

1

Answers

Colons

1. a) There were only two things that Fred worried about: where the colon went and why it was used.

   b) He only needed one thing to get through the week: money.

   c) Rule number one: the teacher is always right.

   d) Everything went right on that day: they won the lottery, the electricity came back on, Jane got a new job, and their pet dog was found.

   e) The teacher walked in and opened her mouth to speak: "Pens down and pay attention to what I am going to say."

2. a)–c) There are many possible answers. Your sentences must include a colon in an appropriate place.

PAGE 11

Apostrophes of omission

1. a) Saffron couldn't believe that she had got the question wrong.

   b) Dean hadn't done his homework.

   c) Kayleigh shouldn't have eaten all the cakes.

   d) "I've got it!" shouted Ryan.

   e) "Where's the exit?" asked Ahmed.

   f) "I could've done that!" remarked Rachel.

   g) "Lucy won't do the reading," explained Miss Sowter.

2. a) I'd b) You'll c) They've d) Don't

Apostrophes of possession

1. a) Joe's pub is in New York.

   b) Nobody understood why Oliver's answer was wrong.

   c) Lots of boys' teams took part in the competition.

   d) Matthew was distracted by the women's chatter.

   e) James' excuse for not doing his homework wasn't accepted by the teacher.

   f) Saira's bag had broken.

   g) The girl's book was returned to her.

2. a) Correct b) Incorrect c) Incorrect

It's and its

1. a) It's / its a nice day for a walk.

   b) The glass had lost it's / its shine.

PAGE 13

Topics and paragraphs

1. a)–b) There are many possible answers. Paragraphs should continue with the topic introduced in the topic sentence and expand on the topic.

Paragraph length

1. There are many possible answers, e.g. Her head rested heavily on her hand. She could barely keep her eyes open, except to keep glancing at the clock to count down the minutes until the end of class. She counted with the second hand – 56, 57, 58, 59, 60.

2. There are many possible answers, e.g. The city is alive with culture and history. There are so many sights to see, so many places to experience, so many restaurants to dine in. The streets bustle with friendly people – locals and tourists – whilst everything basks in glorious sunshine.

PAGE 15

Connectives

1.

a) Firstly	Connective of sequence / order / time
b) So far	Connective of sequence / order / time
c) and	Connective of addition
d) Consequently	Connective of cause / effect
e) in brief	Connective of summary

2. There are many possible answers. Make sure you have used each of the connectives once in an appropriate place.

3. Initially; In addition to; In particular; Apart from.

PAGE 17

Connectives as transitions

1. a) So much for the school work; what about the holidays?

   b) Since we know a great deal about football, let us turn to the subject of hockey.

Answers

c) <u>Although</u> they won the lottery, <u>they also</u> continued to work.

d) <u>Despite</u> eating too much, <u>they still</u> enjoyed the meal.

2. **There are many possible answers, e.g.**

a) In addition to the cold, it was raining; furthermore, a storm was forecast.

b) Besides getting a cold, he also got a rash.

c) In spite of the weather we went for a run, although it wasn't much fun.

d) Despite the high price I bought it; on the other hand it was a bit of a rip off.

Connectives as signposts

1. a) Let's <u>first</u> take a look at what happened.

b) The <u>second</u> problem relates to the views of the government.

c) <u>To begin with</u>, we must review what we know.

d) <u>To conclude</u>, we should consider all the evidence.

e) <u>Initially</u> – <u>and most importantly</u> – there is the matter of who will pay.

Combining connectives and signposts

1. **There are many possible answers. You must include at least one example of a connective, a transition and a signpost.**

PAGE 19

Writing in a consistent voice

1. a) Emily went to school and caught the bus. She ran from the bus-park and entered the school through its main gates. After doing this she was worn out because she had run out of breath. Her teacher was waiting and told her off for coming into the classroom with messy uniform.

b) **There are many possible answers. Make sure you have used the past tense throughout.**

2. buried; Experts; hoard; quoted; ancient.

3. **There are many possible answers, e.g.** slowly; creaking; dark; nervous; terrible; gloomy; reluctantly; muffled; screaming.

PAGE 21

Adjectives

1. **There are many possible answers, e.g. a)** crumpled, family **b)** sparkly, green **c)** constant bad **d)** old unreliable **e)** annoying younger **f)** black designer

Alliteration

1. **There are many possible answers, e.g.**
a) scaly, slippery **b)** tall, twisted **c)** derelict and dilapidated **d)** dazzling diamond **e)** sickly, sweet

Similes

1. **There are many possible answers, e.g.**
a) naughty little **b)** shiny new **c)** thick stodgy **d)** grey stagnant **e)** silly old

2. **There are many possible answers, e.g. a)** that had lost its wallet **b)** that had come from the North Pole **c)** that had been run over **d)** that has never seen the sunshine **e)** that has been in the freezer

PAGE 23

Avoiding clichés and common mistakes

1. **There are many possible answers. Try to use a variety of techniques, e.g. alliteration, adjectives, similes.**

Planning and drafting

1. 1D; 2A; 3E; 4C; 5B

PAGE 25

What are adverbs?

1. a) <u>Annoyingly</u>, Richard was right.

b) Tom <u>fortunately</u> got the message in the nick of time.

c) Ed <u>almost</u> won the lottery.

d) Sandra got her homework done <u>hurriedly</u>.

e) Someone <u>always</u> loses.

f) <u>Surprisingly</u>, Shauna sat next to one of the boys.

g) Fiona ate her dinner <u>lazily</u>.

2. a) quickly **b)** Lazily **c)** accurately **d)** carefully **e)** loudly **f)** aggressively **g)** enthusiastically

Answers

Positioning adverbs

1. There are a number of possible answers, e.g.
   a) Fortunately, Syed was wrong.
   b) Carelessly, Tara gave away the answer away by speaking loudly.
   c) Bob wrote a great article for the newspaper but lost it, stupidly.
   d) Excitedly, Daniel published his pictures.
   e) Francis wins the egg-and-spoon race easily and triumphantly cheers afterwards.

PAGE 27

Using a thesaurus

1. There are many possible answers, e.g.
   a) dreadful b) vast c) beautifully d) awful
   e) ancient f) fracas g) freezing h) superb i) costly

2. a) Brambly b) Apathetic c) Malodorous
   d) Exquisite e) Voluminous f) Diminutive
   g) Geriatric h) Adolescent i) Lustrous

3. a)–e) There are many possible answers. Make sure you understand the meaning of each word and that you have used each word in an appropriate context.

PAGE 29

'Good' words

1. There are many possible answers, e.g.
   a) stupendous b) first-rate c) commendable
   d) honest e) marvellous f) splendid g) wonderful
   h) valuable i) excellent j) charitable

'Bad' words

1. There are many possible answers, e.g.
   a) abominable b) inadequate c) bummer
   d) unacceptable e) lousy f) cruddy g) atrocious
   h) incorrect i) unsatisfactory j) substandard

PAGE 31

Spelling rules

1. a) piece b) brief c) Weigh

2. a) later b) latter c) bitter d) biter

3. a) Raspberry b) February c) Necessity d) Library
   e) Neighbour f) Hypocrisy g) Address
   h) Disappoint i) Business j) Rumour

Syllables and phonemes

1. a) 4; 8 b) 3; 7 c) 1; 3

Root words

1. a) ped b) bio c) chrono

PAGE 33

Adding suffixes

1. a) appalling b) hauled c) formally d) usually
   e) locally f) kidnapped g) occurred

2. a) admitted b) regretted c) benefited d) visited
   e) committed f) visiting g) regretting

Forming plurals

1. a) Writers b) Potatoes c) Cherries d) Monkeys
   e) Beaches f) Brothers-in-law g) Loaves h) Mice
   i) Reefs j) Women k) Elephants l) Rice m) Cacti
   n) Intelligence o) Halves

PAGE 35

Planning

1. There are many possible answers. For example:

b)

New York

Landmarks
Empire State Building – tallest building
Statue of Liberty
Chrysler Building
Rockefellar Centre
Grand Central Station – History
Ground Zero – Emotional
Flat Iron Building

Shopping
Fifth Avenue
Chinatown
Saks
Bloomingdales

Leisure
Central Park – horse-and-carriage ride
Times Square – lively, noisy
Broadway – shows

c)

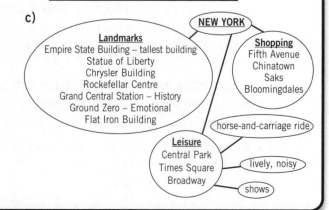

Answers

PAGE 37

Types of formal writing and formal letters

1. 1 – Postal code missing; **2** – Address of the recipient missing; **3** – Date missing;
4 – Inappropriate style, too informal; **5** – Inappropriate style, too informal; **6** – Inappropriate style, too informal; **7** – Signature missing

PAGE 39

Types of informal writing

1. **There are several possible answers, e.g. a)** Are you coming for dinner with me? **b)** From now on, call me Ernest Tubb. **c)** You wouldn't stop me seeing my mum? **d)** The accommodation needs to be cleaned. **e)** I want you to stop!

Informal letters

1. **There are many possible answers, e.g.**

   Hi! Thanks for your email. Crikey, I can't believe that story about Janine – she's as daft as a soggy brush! I was like, 'You've gotta be joking?' when I heard, but after I talked to her I could believe it. She tried to tell me a whole different story – it was a load of rubbish. Wow, what a weird girl! Anyway, do you want to go out Saturday? Where do you want to go? I'm not bothered. Bye for now, Daisy xxx

PAGE 41

Descriptive / story openings

1. **There are many possible openings, e.g.**
   The boat shook violently as the waves battered it incessantly. The fierce froth of the raging sea landed on the fragile decks, drenching us and refusing to let up. I wiped my eyes…
   Make sure your opening includes adjectives, adverbs, alliteration and a variety of sentence types.

Instructional openings

1. **There are many possible openings, e.g.** Unwrap the battery and SIM card and insert them into the back of the phone, as shown. Replace the phone cover…
   Make sure your opening includes imperatives, short sentences and technical vocabulary.

Letter openings

1. **There are many possible openings, e.g.** Dear Mo, How's it going? Do you want to come to Alton Towers with me and my parents on Saturday? It'll be fun. Can't wait to go on the Oblivion – it's the scariest ride ever! You will come, won't you?
   Make sure your opening includes informal vocabulary, a variety of sentence types, exaggeration and a rhetorical question.

2. **There are many possible openings, e.g.** Dear Mrs Oates, I am writing to request that Sarah be excused from attending school on Tuesday 25th due to a hospital appointment…
   Make sure your opening includes an appropriate style, respectful vocabulary and complex sentences.

PAGE 43

Descriptive / story endings

1. **There are many possible endings, e.g.** She nervously wiped the glistening beads of sweat from her forehead then stepped gingerly towards the open door – never to return; never to confess…?

Instructional endings

1. **There are many possible endings, e.g.** When you see the screen showing the company logo, you will have activated the console correctly. For further advice on how to use the game pad, refer to the relevant section of this guide. You are now ready to play your first game.

Letter endings

1. **There are many possible endings, e.g.** Ok, so you'll come. You have to! Snow boarding is just the best! You'll really enjoy it. See you Saturday. Love Chloe xxx

2. **There are many possible endings, e.g.** To conclude then, I am extremely disappointed about the treatment I received. I expect, at the very least, a full apology. I hope to hear from you soon.
   Yours faithfully,
   Jane Martin

Answers

PAGE 45

Structure of texts and structure of sentences

1. 1F; 2B; 3E; 4D; 5C; 6A

2.
The house stood proudly on the hill, battered by the wind and rain; it was waiting for him now.	Conclusion
He took his first step up the hill, his heart in his mouth, wondering what fate awaited him.	Climax
He knocked on the door – it opened and the face he remembered was there in front of him. His heart leapt with excitement.	Introduction
The face frowned. "What are you doing here? I don't want to see you again."	Development paragraph
He turned sadly and trudged off back to where he had started from.	Anti-climax

PAGE 47

Reading between the lines

2–6. There are many possible responses. For example:

2. a) What does this suggest about the mood in the room? What does it suggest about the teaching?	**b)** It implies a dull, uninspiring room and the teaching is uninspiring and dull too.
3. a) What does this suggest about his character? What does it make the reader feel about him?	**b)** It suggests that the speaker is an inflexible dull character, who the reader will not warm to.
4. a) Why might it be like this? What impression might he have on his listeners?	**b)** The speaker's attitude is probably symbolised by his voice – he will probably bore his listeners.
5. a) Why is his head compared to a plum pie? What does this make the reader feel?	**b)** His head is probably misshapen and a bit ugly, again making the reader dislike him.

PAGE 49

Integrating quotations into analysis

1. a) Level 5 because it only makes general comments. It only shows an overall understanding of the quotation. No technical terms are used.

   b) Level 6 because it makes detailed comments on the quotations. It uses appropriate technical vocabulary and it integrates quotations into the explanations.

PAGE 51

Similes and metaphors

1. a) The water was <u>as clear as glass</u>.

   b) Debra looked <u>like she had been slapped with a wet fish</u>.

   c) Gerard's house was <u>like a medieval castle</u>.

   d) Jamie was <u>as angry as a disturbed swarm of bees</u>.

   e) Steve's new musical instrument looked <u>like a magical treasure</u>.

2. a) <u>Time is a thief</u>.

   b) <u>The sky was a huge grey blanket</u>, as the storm started.

   c) <u>The girl's eyes were liquid pools of tears</u> as she started to cry happily.

   d) <u>Words are bullets</u>, because they can hurt you deeply.

   e) <u>The team's victory was a sparkling jewel</u> in their season.

3. a) Simile b) Metaphor c) Simile d) Simile e) Metaphor

Pathetic fallacy and personification

1. a) Pathetic fallacy b) Personification c) Pathetic fallacy d) Personification e) Personification

PAGE 53

Alliteration

1. a) The <u>c</u>razy <u>c</u>ook <u>k</u>icked the apprentice out of the <u>k</u>itchen.

   b) <u>P</u>erfect <u>p</u>erformance by the <u>p</u>ostman was rewarded.

   c) <u>L</u>azy <u>L</u>uke <u>l</u>iked to <u>l</u>ean over.

   d) The <u>t</u>errible <u>t</u>eam <u>tott</u>ered on the brink of relegation.

2. **There are many possible answers, e.g.** I lightly licked my lollipop.

Onomatopoeia

1. a) Boom / bang b) Miaow / purr c) Buzz d) Baa

2. **There are many possible answers, e.g.** The fireworks fizzed then shot up, booming and popping in the sky.

© Letts Educational Ltd

Answers

Assonance, sibilance and consonance

1. a) The gr<u>ou</u>nd res<u>ou</u>nded with the s<u>ou</u>nd of the earthquake.
   b) The b<u>i</u>g t<u>i</u>p is f<u>i</u>lled to the br<u>i</u>m.
   c) The explorers s<u>a</u>dly tr<u>a</u>cked b<u>a</u>ck from the b<u>a</u>d p<u>a</u>th.
   d) Wh<u>o</u> d<u>o</u> y<u>ou</u> think y<u>ou</u> are?

2. **There are many possible answers, e.g.**
   a) We n<u>ee</u>d to s<u>ee</u> the thr<u>ee</u> p<u>eo</u>ple imm<u>e</u>diately.
   b) He mu<u>tt</u>ered some u<u>tt</u>erances and wen<u>t</u> <u>t</u>o bed.
   c) I wi<u>sh</u> <u>sh</u>e'd <u>sh</u>are her <u>s</u>ugary <u>s</u>weet<u>s</u>.

PAGE 55

Juxtaposition and oxymoron

1. a) Humour b) Comparison / contrast
   c) Comparison / contrast d) Humour
   e) Comparison / contrast

2. **There are many possible answers, e.g.** Cold fire; bitter sweet

Hyperbole

1. **There are many possible answers, e.g.**
   a) I am more angry and annoyed than I have ever been before in my entire life!
   b) It is the tallest building in the whole world.
   c) My bedroom is always the messiest room in the house.
   d) I would feel incredibly, amazingly excited – too excited for words!

Imagery

1. Desert imagery.

PAGE 57

Rhyme patterns and internal rhyme

1. a) i) AABBA ii) Limerick
   b) i) AABB ii) Rhyming couplets
   c) i) ABCB ii) Simple four line
   d) i) ABBA ii) Enclosed rhyme
   e) i) AABA ii) Rubaiyat

PAGE 59

Rhythm in poetry and common rhythm patterns

1. Ten
2. It means rhythm.
3. Two syllables, with only the first stressed.
4. Three syllables, with only the third stressed.
5. One stressed syllable followed by two unstressed.
6. Two consecutive syllables that are both stressed.
7. Spondee
8. a) Iambic pentameter b) Trochee c) Spondee
   d) Dactyl
9. a) There are many possible answers. Your answer must contain two lines of five syllables in alternate unstressed syllable, stressed syllable, unstressed syllable, stressed syllable...
   b) There are many possible answers. Your line must contain two syllables, with only the first one stressed.
   c) There are many possible answers. Your line must contain three syllables, with only the third syllable stressed.
   d) There are many possible answers. Your line must contain one stressed syllable immediately followed by two unstressed syllables.
   e) There are many possible answers. Your line must contain two consecutive syllables that are both stressed.

PAGE 61

Genre

1. a) Action-adventure b) Romance c) Fantasy

Typical features of genres

1. a) Science fiction b) Horror c) Cowboy / Wild West / Western d) Crime e) Romance

Answers

PAGE 63

Literature before Shakespeare

1. **There are many possible answers, e.g.**

    a) Lived 672 / 673–May 26, 735; Buried in Durham cathedral; Wrote *The History of the English Church* and *The History of the English People*

    b) Written by an unknown author; Poem; Probably an oral poem originally.

    c) Written by an unknown author; Possibly written in North Staffordshire; Dates from the 14th century.

Shakespeare and his contemporaries

1. **There are many possible answers, e.g.**

    a) Lived 30 November 1554–17 October 1586; Poet, courtier and soldier; Wrote *Astrophel and Stella*.

    b) Wrote *Tamburlaine*; Born in Canterbury; Was murdered.

    c) Lived 11 June 1572–6 August 1637; Wrote poems and plays; Wrote *The Alchemist*.

    d) Lived 1552–1599; Wrote *The Faerie Queene*; Was called a 'poet's poet'.

    e) Wrote metaphysical poems; Was also a preacher; Wrote religious and romantic poems.

    f) Over 100 written; Some written to a 'dark lady'; Some written to a rival poet.

    g) 38 written; History, tragedy, comedy plays; Last plays / some parts were possibly not written by Shakespeare.

PAGE 65

Literature after Shakespeare

1. **There are many possible answers, e.g.**

    a) Brother and sister; lived in and inspired by the Lake District; Buried in Grasmere.

    b) Based on a dream; Raised scientific ideas of cloning; Published when Mary Shelley was 20.

    c) Was an acquaintance of the poet Shelley; Died in Rome; Wrote famous poems called 'Odes', e.g. *Ode to Autumn*.

    d) Contains characters, Darcy and Elizabeth Bennet; First published in 1813; Originally called 'First Impressions'.

    e) Many were written to her sister Cassandra; Some were destroyed relating to a possibly sad part of her life; Reveal her sarcastic humour.

    f) Partly based on Charlotte's own experiences; Mr Rochester is the main male character; Jane is a governess.

    g) Regarded as coarse by Victorian readers; Heathcliff is the main male character; Contains gothic features.

    h) Inspired by the moors around Haworth; First published under the name of Ellis Bell; Published a joint collection of poetry with her sisters.

    i) Criticised Victorian ideas of education; Dickens' tenth novel; First published in a publication called *Household Words*.

    j) Main characters are George and Lennie; Based on travelling workers; Set in California during the Depression.

PAGE 67

Audience, purpose and content

These are practical exercises – there are no answers.

PAGE 69

Listening and making good notes

These are practical exercises – there are no answers.

PAGE 71

Effective speaking and non-verbal cues

These are practical exercises – there are no answers.

Published by Letts Educational Ltd.
An imprint of HarperCollins*Publishers*

Text © 2010 Nick Barber
Design and illustration © 2010 Letts Educational Ltd

Types of formal writing and formal letters

❶ Look at the short formal letter below. Some missing or incorrect features are numbered and marked in red. Fill in the table at the bottom of the page explaining what is wrong or what is missing from the features marked.

50 Art Street

Chichester

West Sussex

❶

❷

❸

Dear Sir,

I wish to purchase a painting from you. I visited your exhibition at the Fulks' gallery in Chicago and was very impressed with one painting entitled 'Mars Cheese Castle'. As I understand, this was on sale for £6000.

If the painting is still available and unsold, I would like to formally register my interest. If you are willing to sell the painting, please contact me at the earliest possible opportunity. ❹ I'd love to see it hanging up in my living room; don't you think that'd be brill?

❺ Yours truly

❻ Lots of love

❼

Mr Robbie Giersoe

1)	
2)	
3)	
4)	
5)	
6)	
7)	

7

Informal writing

Types of informal writing

There are many types of informal writing. Some of the more common types that you might come across include the following:

- Emails
- Websites
- Blog posts
- Letters to / from friends and family

Informal writing differs from formal writing in many ways, for example:

- It can be structured in more varied and unusual ways than formal writing, for example in stories and descriptions.
- It can make use of a much wider range of vocabulary and language techniques, e.g. slang, non-standard grammar.
- It can use a much wider range of viewpoints.
- Abbreviations and slang are more likely to be appropriate for some forms of informal writing.
- Contractions are much more readily accepted in informal writing.

Be careful with informal writing: just because it is much more flexible than formal writing does not mean that you can write anything you like and get away with it. Think of your audience and the purpose of your writing at all times.

Informal letters

Informal letters are letters that you might write to friends or close family, people who you know well. This means that you have more flexibility in how you set out and write the letter.

- There should be an address to which you are writing and your return address should be included too.
- There should be a date indicating when you wrote the letter – this is still useful in an informal letter.
- The salutation can be friendly and short, e.g. 'Hi!', 'Greetings, mate', 'Andy!', but there should always be a salutation of some sort.
- The ending can take a variety of forms. It could just be your name or it could be a friendly final comment, e.g. 'Write soon', 'Hugs', 'See you Friday', but there should be an ending of some sort.
- Slang and abbreviations can be used – how much depends on how well you know the other person and whether they are likely to understand you.

Always make sure that the person you are writing to knows you well enough to understand how you write, and will understand the vocabulary and abbreviations that you might want to use. What might be easy and clear for you might not be easy and clear for the person reading it to understand.

Writing

Learn

Types of informal writing

1 Here are a number of formal sentences. Change them so that they become more informal and personal. They can be re-written in a variety of ways.

> **Example**
> **Formal:** I would like to request your company this evening.
> **Informal:** Do you want to come out with me tonight?

a) **Formal:** Would you do me the honour of attending the dinner with me?

   Informal: _____

b) **Formal:** Henceforth I shall be known as Ernest Tubb.

   Informal: _____

c) **Formal:** Would you deny me the opportunity to visit my mother?

   Informal: _____

d) **Formal:** The accommodation would have benefited from sanitary improvement.

   Informal: _____

e) **Formal:** I would like to request that you desist.

   Informal: _____

5

Informal letters

1 Write a short e-mail to a friend, using an informal style. You must use each of the words and phrases in the table once. There are several ways that this might be done.

Hi
You've gotta be joking?
Bye for now
Crikey
As daft as a soggy brush
I'm not bothered
A load of rubbish
Wow

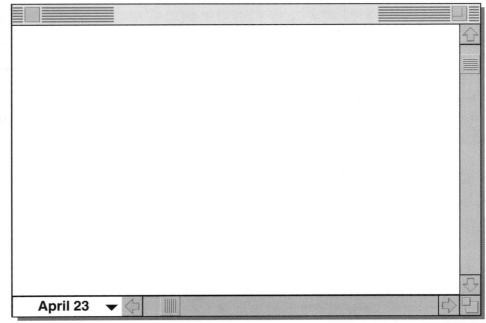

April 23

8

Total marks   13

Creating effective openings

Writing

Learn

Descriptive / story openings

To create an effective opening, a writer must think about the **audience** and the **purpose** of the writing. If you are writing the opening of a novel or story, you want to get the reader's attention, so they carry on reading. Depending on the reader's age and interests you can use different techniques.

Example – This opening uses adjectives, adverbs, alliteration, a rhetorical question and complex sentences to create a description.

Elizabeth stared thoughtfully out to sea, beyond the pier, beyond the waves pattering gently on the beach below. She had been there a long time, but she was oblivious. Oblivious to the time quickly passing, to the bustle of people behind her, and to the man's presence. He gazed longingly at her soft, silky hair as it was blown gently by the breeze. He wanted to say something – but could he?

Audience – teenagers or older   **Purpose** – to entertain, romantic fiction

Instructional openings

If you are writing the opening of a set of instructions, you would want to make the purpose of the instructions clear. You would use vocabulary that is suitable for the kind of person who wants to follow the instructions.

Example – This opening uses short sentences, imperatives, a personal tone and technical vocabulary to create instructional writing.

By following these instructions, you will quickly be able to use your new camera.
Unpack the padding that surrounds the camera. Remove all sticky tape. Find the button marked 'Stabiliser'. Ensure it is set to 'Off'. Then insert the camera battery in the battery compartment.

Audience – all ages (but assuming some basic knowledge of cameras)   **Purpose** – to instruct, instructional writing

Letter openings

If you are writing the opening of a letter, you need to think about the purpose. You must consider how well you know the person you are writing to, because this will affect how you address them.

Example – This opening uses a formal tone, complex sentences, and respectful vocabulary.

Dear Sir or Madam,
With regard to your enquiry regarding the hire of the hall, we would like to provide you with the hire costs for such an undertaking. All our costs include full insurance and tax.

Audience – an adult customer, someone you do not know well   **Purpose** – to inform, provide factual information

Remember 'www dot' rhymes with 'Who? Why? What?' – the '3 Ws'. When writing an opening you must ask yourself: **Who** *am I writing for?* **Why** *am I writing it?* **What** *am I writing?*

Key words   rhetorical question • imperative • complex sentence

Descriptive / story openings

1 Write the opening paragraph of an adventure story for teenagers or adults. Use adjectives, adverbs, alliteration and a variety of sentence types. Continue on a separate sheet of paper if necessary.

_____

_____

_____

4

Instructional openings

1 Write the opening of a set of instructions for a new phone. Use imperatives, short sentences and technical vocabulary. Continue on a separate sheet of paper if necessary.

_____

_____

_____

3

Letter openings

1 Write the opening of an informal letter to a friend, inviting them to spend a day out with you and your family. Use informal vocabulary, a variety of sentence types, exaggeration and a rhetorical question. Continue on a separate sheet of paper if necessary.

_____

_____

_____

_____

2 Write the opening of a formal letter to a school teacher asking permission for a child to have a day off school. Use an appropriate style, respectful vocabulary and complex sentences. Continue on a separate sheet of paper if necessary.

_____

_____

_____

_____

7

Total marks   14

Creating effective endings

Writing

Learn

Descriptive / story endings

To write an effective ending you need to ask yourself some questions:
- Do you want to reveal everything or leave some things to the imagination of the reader?
- Do you want to shock, surprise or create other feelings?

Example
This is a descriptive ending, which uses ellipsis, adjectives and varied sentences:

She stopped. She turned. It all came flooding back now – why hadn't she realised before? There was only one thing to do and that was to go back again...

Audience – teenagers or older   **Purpose** – to entertain and conclude, but leave some things to the imagination.

 Avoid clichés like, 'Then I woke up and it was all a dream'.

Instructional endings

An effective ending to instructions should give a sense of what should have been achieved or created. For example, if the instructions were for making a model, the ending should give some indication of what the model should look like.

Example
This is the ending of a set of instructions for a new toaster. It uses short sentences, imperatives, a personal tone and technical vocabulary:

A 'ping' sound will indicate that the toast is ready. Place the bread back in the slots if you wish to toast it for longer, repeating stages 2 and 3 of these instructions. Keep it clean to prolong its life.

Audience – any user of the toaster   **Purpose** – to explain / instruct how to use the toaster

Letter endings

Letter endings can be formal or informal and will vary depending on purpose, e.g. a strong formal letter of complaint would be more forcefully ended than a formal request to hire a venue.

Example
This is a formal ending to a letter requesting a replacement washing machine. It uses a respectful tone, a rhetorical question and adjectives:

I think that it would only be reasonable that the broken washing machine should be replaced, free of charge – don't you? It didn't work from the moment it was delivered, so was obviously faulty before it reached me. I look forward to your prompt reply and commitment to replace the goods.

Yours faithfully

Audience – a complaints department (adults)   **Purpose** – to persuade, to obtain a refund.

Key words   ellipsis • tone

Descriptive / story endings

1 Write the final paragraph of a mystery story, without giving away what happened, but by dropping hints through the description and punctuation. Continue on a separate sheet of paper if necessary.

_____

_____

_____

4

Instructional endings

1 Write the final part of the instructions for a new games console, assuming that the person reading has never played or used one before. Continue on a separate sheet of paper if necessary.

_____

_____

_____

4

Letter endings

1 Write the ending of a letter to a friend, in which you have tried to persuade them to do an extreme sports activity! Continue on a separate sheet of paper if necessary.

_____

_____

_____

_____

2 Write the ending of a formal letter, in which you complain about the treatment that you received at a popular theme park when you lost your glasses on one of the rides. Continue on a separate sheet of paper if necessary.

_____

_____

_____

_____

8

Structure

Structure of texts

At Level 6, you will be expected to have an understanding of the **structure** of a text and be able to comment on it. Structure in writing can involve many things:

- It can be the overall shape and organisation of a piece of writing.
- It can be the overall shape and organisation of a section of writing.
- It can relate to the position of sentences in a paragraph.
- It can relate to the position of words within a sentence.
- It might involve the use of deliberate contrasts.

An extended piece of writing should have certain structural features. These include an introduction or opening to establish the writing; a main purpose, central focus or **climax** and a conclusion or appropriate ending.

In the middle of a piece of writing, there can be many parts, depending on the type of writing:

- There might be a climax – the peak, the main point, the most exciting or important part of the writing.
- There might be an **anti-climax** – this will be a contrast to the climax, where the mood changes after the climax.
- There may be a **thesis** – a proposition or idea that is put forward.
- There will be paragraphs of development, where main ideas are taken further.

There may also be other parts to the writing; the ones listed above are some of the more common features.

Structure of sentences

The order of sentences within paragraphs, and the order of words within sentences, can have a big effect on the writing and the readers' responses.

In a paragraph, the opening sentence is usually a **topic sentence**, which in some way introduces the ideas in the paragraph.

Sentences may be arranged in various ways after the topic sentence. They can develop, contrast, explore and argue different ideas. They might be used to build up to a mini-climax, or to increase tension.

The words within the sentences are also arranged to achieve particular effects, for example, certain words may be brought to the beginning of the sentence for emphasis.

Key words   structure • climax • anti-climax • thesis

Structure of texts and structure of sentences

1 The paragraphs in the table below are in the wrong order. Put the paragraphs in the correct order by writing the letters next to the paragraph numbers.

	Paragraph
A	So, in conclusion, I ask you to consider what I have already done for the school and vote for me, so that I can continue the work that I feel still needs to be done.
B	In addition to what I have done for the school, I have carried out a lot of charity work outside of school hours, including a whole year working voluntarily at a care home.
C	An example of these far-fetched ideas is the proposal to have flat-screen TVs and game consoles in the common rooms for wet breaks. My ideas are much more reasonable, won't cost the school a fortune and will actually have a chance of happening.
D	As well as being a risk, I also think that some of the policies put forward by the other candidates are far-fetched and not achievable.
E	In contrast to my voluntary work, the other candidates standing have demonstrated very little commitment to the school or to the community. I feel that it would be a big risk if you voted for them.
F	To begin, I feel I should outline the main reasons why I am standing for the school council. I have served the council in previous years and have always been commended on what I have done for the school.

1 _____ 2 _____ 3 _____

4 _____ 5 _____ 6 _____

2 Look at the short story below. The sentences are in the correct order, but the names of the parts of the story are not. Draw lines to link each sentence to the correct part of the story.

Sentence	Part of story
The house stood proudly on the hill, battered by the wind and rain; it was waiting for him now.	Conclusion
He took his first step up the hill, his heart in his mouth, wondering what fate awaited him.	Climax
He knocked on the door – it opened and the face he remembered was there in front of him. His heart leapt with excitement.	Introduction
The face frowned. "What are you doing here? I don't want to see you again."	Development paragraph
He turned sadly and trudged off back to where he had started from.	Anti-climax

11

Total marks 11

45

Practise

Reading

Studying texts

Reading between the lines

The skill of reading between the lines is something that you are expected to do before you reach Level 6 in your reading, but you need to develop this skill to progress through Level 6.

Reading between the lines can be developed by learning to question the text in front of you. Look at this extract from *Shakespeare's Romeo and Juliet*:

TYBALT:	What, art thou drawn among these heartless hinds?
	Turn thee, Benvolio, look upon thy death.
BENVOLIO:	I do but keep the peace. Put up thy sword,
	Or manage it to part these men with me.
TYBALT:	What, drawn, and talk of peace! I hate the word,
	As I hate hell, all Montagues, and thee.
	Have at thee, coward!

When reading this extract, you might ask yourself the following questions:
- What sort of **mood** is Tybalt in?
- Which words give clues towards his mood?
- Which punctuation gives clues towards his mood?
- What sort of mood is Benvolio in?
- Which words give clues towards his mood?
- What do the different moods of the two characters suggest about their relationship?

Reading between the lines is all about asking yourself questions about the text and then thinking of different ways that those questions could be answered. You will find that the answers to one set of questions prompts further questions, which will lead to more detailed study of the text.

Here are some responses to the questions above and further questions that they raise:
- What sort of mood is Tybalt in?
  An angry, violent mood. ⟶ Why is he in this mood?
- Which words give clues towards his mood?
  'Turn thee', 'look upon thy death'. ⟶ Why does he keep using commands? What else does this suggest about his character?
- Which punctuation gives clues towards his mood?
  Exclamation marks. ⟶ Why does Tybalt's character need to use so many? What does this suggest about how angry he is?
- What sort of mood is Benvolio in?
  A calm, peace-keeping mood. ⟶ Why does he feel the need to be peace-keeping? Is this his normal character?
- Which words give clues towards his mood?
  'I do but keep the peace'. ⟶ Why is he almost apologising? What does this suggest about how he feels towards Tybalt?
- What do the different moods of the two characters suggest about their relationship?
  They don't get on. ⟶ Why don't they get on? What is behind this?

At Level 6, you need to keep asking questions like this to develop your analytical skills – and try to find answers to your questions from the details of the text.

Key words   mood

a) Think of two questions that you might ask yourself about each of the underlined parts of the text below. The first one is done for you as an example, in the table underneath the passage.

b) Then write down suggested answers to your questions, in the third column.

"NOW, what I want is, Facts. Teach these boys and girls nothing but Facts. Facts alone are wanted in life ❶. Plant nothing else, and root out everything else. You can only form the minds of reasoning animals upon Facts: nothing else will ever be of any service to them. This is the principle on which I bring up my own children, and this is the principle on which I bring up these children. Stick to Facts, sir!"

The scene was a plain, bare, monotonous vault of a schoolroom ❷, and the speaker's square forefinger emphasized his observations by underscoring every sentence with a line on the schoolmaster's sleeve. The emphasis was helped by the speaker's square wall of a forehead ❸, which had his eyebrows for its base, while his eyes found commodious cellarage in two dark caves, overshadowed by the wall. The emphasis was helped by the speaker's mouth, which was wide, thin, and hard set. The emphasis was helped by the speaker's voice, which was inflexible, dry, and dictatorial ❹. The emphasis was helped by the speaker's hair, which bristled on the skirts of his bald head, a plantation of firs to keep the wind from its shining surface, all covered with knobs, like the crust of a plum pie ❺, as if the head had scarcely warehouse-room for the hard facts stored inside. The speaker's obstinate carriage, square coat, square legs, square shoulders, — nay, his very neckcloth, trained to take him by the throat with an unaccommodating grasp, like a stubborn fact, as it was, — all helped the emphasis.

From *Hard Times* by Charles Dickens

❶ 'Facts alone are wanted in life.'	**a)** *Why does the speaker say this? What sort of character does this suggest he has?*	**b)** *Because he is very opinionated. It suggests that he is a bit dull.*
❷ 'The scene was a plain, bare, monotonous vault of a schoolroom,'	**a)** _____ _____ _____	**b)** _____ _____ _____
❸ 'the speaker's square wall of a forehead'	**a)** _____ _____ _____	**b)** _____ _____ _____
❹ 'the speaker's voice, which was inflexible, dry, and dictatorial'	**a)** _____ _____ _____	**b)** _____ _____ _____
❺ 'like the crust of a plum pie,'	**a)** _____ _____ _____	**b)** _____ _____ _____

8

Total marks 8

Using quotations

Reading

Learn

Integrating quotations into analysis

When you are writing about **quotations**, you need to be able to develop more than straightforward ideas if you want to progress through Level 6.

Here is an example of a 'Point – Quote – Comment' from an essay on *Romeo and Juliet* that shows features of **Level 5**.

> The first thing we learn about Romeo is that he is confused:
> "Feather of lead, bright smoke, cold fire, sick health!
> Still-waking sleep, that is not what it is!
> This love feel I, that feel no love in this."
> In this quotation, Romeo uses lots of contrasting ideas which show that he does not know what to think and so he is quite mixed up.

To improve this part of the essay so it shows features of **Level 6**, the writer needs to do the following:
- Name the techniques that the writer is using more precisely.
- Develop more detailed opinions.
- Integrate quotations into the explanation.

These features need to be carried out consistently throughout the full essay.

Here is the same point again, re-written, to show more features of Level 6:

> Romeo, when he first appears, shows signs of confusion by using oxymorons such as 'Feather of lead, bright smoke, sick health'. By using a range of contrasting ideas like this, the audience gets to see Romeo's emotional confusion. When he says, 'This love feel I, that feel no love in this' the juxtaposition of the two parts of the phrase do not seem to make sense, which implies that Romeo himself cannot make sense of what is in his head and his heart. By using several oxymorons in one speech, the cumulative effect is one of great confusion and the audience can only assume that it is about a woman who does not love him.

This response shows features of Level 6 because:
- The writer is far more precise in naming the techniques used. Words such as '**oxymoron**' and '**juxtaposition**' show this.
- The opinions given are more detailed. The writer has picked out individual parts of a longer quotation to show exactly where he / she has got his / her ideas from, rather than making a general comment about the quotation as a whole, which the first writer did.
- Quotations are integrated into the sentences, so that the writing is easier to read and the ideas flow more smoothly and clearly.

> *Try to use the PEE (Point, Evidence, Explanation) technique when using quotations in your writing:*
> **P**oint – *make a point.*
> **E**vidence – *give the quotation.*
> **E**xplanation – *explain what the quotation shows.*

Key words   quotation • oxymoron • juxtaposition

Integrating quotations into analysis

1 a) Read the extract from an essay below. Say whether you think it shows more features of Level 5 or Level 6 and explain why.

> The first time we meet Juliet, she respects her mother:
> 'I'll look to like, if looking liking move:
> But no more deep will I endart mine eye
> Than your consent gives strength to make it fly.'
>
> This quotation makes the audience feel that Juliet is being well-behaved because of how she speaks to her mother. She uses polite words which show respect.

I think that this shows features of Level _____ because _____

_____

_____

_____

_____

_____

_____

b) Read the extract from another essay below. Say whether you think it shows more features of Level 5 or Level 6 and explain why.

> Juliet's first speech of any length to her mother in Act 1 Scene 3 shows cautious vocabulary such as 'I'll look to like, if looking liking move'. The fact that Juliet uses a conjunction like 'if' to qualify her opinion implies to the audience that she is being careful. She seems as though she does not want to offend her mother. This is further supported when she says that she will respect her mother's 'consent'. The use of this noun suggests that she is used to following commands; not surprising, when we have been told already that she is only 13 years old.

I think that this shows features of Level _____ because _____

_____

_____

_____

_____

_____

_____

8

Total marks 8

Language techniques 1

When you are analysing texts, you need to use the appropriate vocabulary so you can show that you understand the ideas that you are writing or talking about. It will also make explanations much clearer and more precise.

Similes and metaphors

Similes
A **simile** is a comparison technique that normally includes the word 'like' or 'as'.

For example:
- The room was **like** a pig-sty.
- The clouds looked **like** small, fluffy balls of cotton wool.

Metaphors
A **metaphor** is a direct comparison technique, where one thing is said to be, or have the qualities of, something else.
For example:
- The room **was** a pig-sty.
- The clouds **were** small, fluffy balls of cotton wool.

Similes are not as strong as metaphors, because they are not direct comparisons. Similes can sometimes be rather clichéd if not well-thought-out.

Metaphors are often used in descriptive writing, for example in an opening or in a climactic scene.

Pathetic fallacy and personification

Pathetic fallacy and **personification** are similar techniques. Both are comparisons in which human qualities are given to inanimate or non-human features or objects.

Pathetic fallacy
Pathetic fallacy is a technique where human emotions are given to non-human things. For example:
- The clouds cried tears of rain.

Personification
Personification is a technique where other human qualities are given to non-human things. For example:
- The chair jumped across the room.

It is acceptable, when writing about pathetic fallacy and personification, to say that pathetic fallacy is a type of personification.

Key words   simile • metaphor • pathetic fallacy • personification

Similes and metaphors

1 Underline the simile in each of these sentences.

a) The water was as clear as glass.

b) Debra looked like she had been slapped with a wet fish.

c) Gerard's house was like a medieval castle.

d) Jamie was as angry as a disturbed swarm of bees.

e) Steve's new musical instrument looked like a magical treasure.

2 Underline the metaphor in each of these sentences.

a) Time is a thief.

b) The sky was a huge grey blanket, as the storm started.

c) The girl's eyes were liquid pools of tears as she started to cry happily.

d) Words are bullets, because they can hurt you deeply.

e) The team's victory was a sparkling jewel in their season.

3 Write down whether each of the following sentences contains a simile or a metaphor.

a) The sky was as black as coal. _____

b) The sky was a black, oily sheet above their heads. _____

c) The sky looked like a black oily sheet above their heads. _____

d) The sparkling jewellery shone as brightly as a summer sky. _____

e) The little boy was a bright ray of sunshine. _____

15

Pathetic fallacy and personification

1 Write down whether each of the following sentences is an example of personification or pathetic fallacy.

a) The sun smiled happily over us. _____

b) The picture leapt off the wall. _____

c) Nature was happy in the springtime. _____

d) The bus spluttered and stopped. _____

e) The arms of the tree reached out to me. _____

5

Total marks   20

Language techniques 2

Alliteration

Whereas some techniques are used to create a visual impact, other techniques are used to create or describe sound effects in writing.

Alliteration is a technique where words that are close together within a sentence begin with the same letter or sound. Alliteration is used to create different kinds of effects, depending on the sound of the common letters, for example, whether they are hard or soft sounding. For example:

- Billy's big ball bounced harmlessly out of the way.
  In this example, the 'b' sound is a round, soft sound which echoes and imitates the movement of the ball.
- The cackling kids created chaos in the classroom.
  In this example, the 'c' / 'k' is a harder sound that echoes and imitates the disruptive mood.

When writing about alliteration, it helps to say the words out loud to give you an idea of whether the sound is hard or soft. You can then work out what sort of effect is being created.

Onomatopoeia

Onomatopoeia refers to when a word sounds like the thing that it is describing. For example:
- The ducks quacked loudly and the cows mooed.

The word 'quack' is an example of onomatopoeia because when the word is pronounced, it resembles the sound of a duck quacking. The word 'moo' is also an example of onomatopoeia because when the word is pronounced, it resembles the sound of a cow mooing.

Other examples of onomatopoeia include 'boom', 'crack' and 'shatter'.

Onomatopoeia is a technique that is often used in writing for younger children, or to create sharp, sudden effects in other writing. If it is used too often, it can lose its impact.

Assonance, sibilance and consonance

Assonance is the repetition of similar vowel sounds. For example:
- Round and down they fell to the ground.

Consonance is the repetition of consonant sounds, in words that are positioned close together in a sentence. For example:
- The flashing feet of the tough fighter went off in another direction.

Sibilance is the repetition of 's' or 'sh' sounds in words that are positioned close together in a sentence. They create a sharp, hissing sound. For example:
- The soft, stuttering sounds caused by the shattered shutters spiced up the night-time.

Key words   alliteration • onomatopoeia • assonance • consonance • sibilance

Alliteration

1. Underline the alliteration in these sentences.

   a) The crazy cook kicked the apprentice out of the kitchen.

   b) Perfect performance by the postman was rewarded.

   c) Lazy Luke liked to lean over.

   d) The terrible team tottered on the brink of relegation.

2. Write a sentence that contains alliteration, using the letter 'l' at least three times.

_____

5

Onomatopoeia

1. Write the onomatopoeic word that matches with the description.

   a) The sound made by an explosion.   _____

   b) The sound made by a cat.   _____

   c) The sound made by a bee.   _____

   d) The sound made by a sheep.   _____

2. Write a sentence that contains onomatopoeia.

_____

5

Assonance, sibilance and consonance

1. Underline the examples of assonance in these sentences.

   a) The ground resounded with the sound of the earthquake.

   b) The big tip is filled to the brim.

   c) The explorers sadly tracked back from the bad path.

   d) Who do you think you are?

2. Write sentences of your own, following the instructions given.

   a) Write a sentence that contains assonance, using at least three examples of an 'e' sound.

   _____

   b) Write a sentence that contains consonance, using at least three examples of a 't' sound.

   _____

   c) Write a sentence that contains sibilance, using at least three examples of 's' or 'sh' sounds.

   _____

7

Practise

Reading

Total marks   17

53

Language techniques 3

Reading

Learn

Juxtaposition and oxymoron

Juxtaposition is the deliberate placing of different elements close together, or in sequence, in order to create a particular effect. For example:

- Tim was the tallest boy in the class. Melanie, however, was the smallest girl.

By juxtaposing these facts, in this order, the effect is to highlight how small Melanie is, in comparison to Tim.

Juxtaposition can be used to create humour, or to shock.

One type of juxtaposition or contrast is known as **oxymoron**. When opposing ideas are placed next to each other, for example, to create a sense of confusion, it is referred to as oxymoron. A famous example is Romeo's use of oxymoron in *Romeo and Juliet* where he uses phrases such as:

> 'O brawling love! O loving hate!
> O anything of nothing first create!
> O heavy lightness, serious vanity!
> Misshapen chaos of well-seeming forms!
> Feather of lead, bright smoke, cold fire, sick health!'

Hyperbole

Hyperbole is the term used to describe extreme exaggeration. It can be used to shock, to provide humour or to emphasise key points. For example:

- There was huge, tumultuous applause that could be heard for miles when John won the tiddlywinks competition.

Imagery

Imagery is the name given to the set of pictures that are created in the reader's mind by a combination of techniques. Writers use connected ideas to create a strong, consistent picture or feeling in a reader's mind. For example:

- The cars shone like stars as they hurtled like comets along the city streets. Meteor trails of red lights shot through the darkness as unknown travellers sped through the universe of night-time.

In this example, lots of references are made to outer space and stars in order to create an overall image / feeling of spectacular adventure to unknown places. This overall imagery of space helps the reader to visualise the scene of fast cars and lights in a city at night.

Key words   juxtaposition • oxymoron • hyperbole • imagery

Juxtaposition and oxymoron

1 Here are some sentences in which different ideas are juxtaposed. Tick the column which relates to the main effect of the juxtaposition.

	Humour	Comparison / contrast
a) The bypass was going to knock down the town hall, the swimming pool and my nan's outside toilet.	☐	☐
b) Mike was tall – so was Sally.	☐	☐
c) Black clouds, bright sunshine – a bad combination.	☐	☐
d) The squeaky voice and the floppy haircut; were they his best qualities?	☐	☐
e) Old tracks, modern highways – which are better?	☐	☐

2 Write an example of an oxymoron.

_____

6

Hyperbole

1 Write four sentences using hyperbole to describe the following.

a) How strongly you feel about being given triple Maths homework one night.

_____

b) How tall a skyscraper is.

_____

c) How messy your bedroom is.

_____

d) How excited you might feel if your family won the lottery.

_____

4

Imagery

1 Read the passage below. What overall image is used to describe the girl and the situation?

The exam started and Becky's mind was a barren desert of information. It seemed wind had blown dust into her brain cells, and tumble-weed and cacti filled her thoughts instead of useful facts and information. She could feel the oppressive sandy heat inside her head. She knew this exam was not going to go well.

_____

1

Total marks 11

Rhyme

Rhyme patterns

If you are studying poetry, then you will need to understand and be able to use vocabulary to describe and comment on features such as **rhyme**.

A lot of poetry has some sort of a rhyme pattern. Sometimes, poetry does not have a pattern at all, in which case it does not rhyme.

Rhyme patterns are written as a series of letters. Look at this example:

Bertie Bullfrog lived by a road	A
He was often mistaken for a toad	A
Just because he was green and black	B
And had huge lumps on his oily back	B

The first two lines rhyme; they are labelled AA. The second two lines also rhyme, but they are a different rhyme, so they are labelled BB. So, you would say that this poem has an AABB rhyme pattern. Two lines that rhyme in an AA or BB pattern are called **rhyming couplets**.

Examples of rhyme patterns
Different rhyme patterns have different names, or different poems follow certain patterns.

For example:
- **Limericks** follow the pattern AABBA.
- Many Shakespearean **sonnets** have the pattern ABAB CDCD EFEF GG.

Some common rhyme patterns are shown in the table:

Pattern	Name
ABBA	Enclosed rhyme
AABA	Rubaiyat
ABABB	Cinquain
ABABBCC	Rhyme Royal
ABCB	Simple four line

Many writers invent their own rhyme pattern to suit a particular mood or purpose, so it is possible to come across many varieties of rhyme pattern.

Internal rhyme

As well as rhyme at the ends of lines, rhyme can take place within lines. This is called **internal rhyme**. For example:
- While I waited, feeling **sad**, my future seemed rather **bad**.

Internal rhyme can be mixed with rhyme at the end of lines, to speed up the poem or create rhythm.

💡 *When writing about rhyme, don't just describe the rhyme; always discuss why it is used as well.*

Key words   rhyme • rhyming couplet • limerick • sonnet • internal rhyme

Rhyme patterns and internal rhyme

1 Read each of these poems and think about what type of rhyme pattern each one has. Then fill in the spaces in the sentences below to complete the descriptions of each poem.

a) *There was a young man from Stoke*
Who wrote some books as a joke
He said "I'm a teacher,
Not a judge, nor a preacher
And it's only because I am broke!"

    i) The rhyme pattern of this poem is _____

    ii) This pattern is called _____

b) *The ship roamed over the mighty sea*
Drifting off to the land of the free
No-one knew if it was safe and sound
Or whether it had sunk on coastal ground.

    i) The rhyme pattern of this poem is _____

    ii) This pattern is called _____

c) *Britney was a silly girl*
She always used to chatter
Until one day she lost her voice
So could no longer natter

    i) The rhyme pattern of this poem is _____

    ii) This pattern is called _____

d) *"Next train's here!" said the Voice*
"It's not late
And it's on Platform Eight
But hurry if your name's Joyce!"

    i) The rhyme pattern of this poem is _____

    ii) This pattern is called _____

e) *The warrior rode over the mighty hill*
With many more miles to fill
He wanted to reach the oasis by night –
Urged on by his fearsome will.

    i) The rhyme pattern of this poem is _____

    ii) This pattern is called _____

10

Rhythm

Rhythm in poetry

Rhythm is another very important feature to consider when writing about poetry.

Writers make use of different rhythms – sometimes within the same poem – to achieve a variety of different effects.

Different rhythms have different names. It helps to know some of these names when you are writing about rhythm.

Rhythm – sometimes called **meter** – is often described using two words:
- The first word describes the sound of the rhythm. For example, the term '**iambic**' describes a rhythm where an unstressed syllable is followed by a stressed syllable.
- The second word refers to how many times the rhythmic pattern repeats within a line. For example, '**pentameter**' means that a pattern repeats five times.

'**Iambic pentameter**', therefore, describes five sets of unstressed / stressed syllables in one line. These sets are sometimes also called **feet**.

Read the following example from John Keats' poem, *Ode to Autumn*. These lines use iambic pentameter.

˘ /	˘ /	˘ /	˘ /	˘ /
To swell	the gourd,	and plump	the ha-	zel shells

Key
˘ stands for an unstressed syllable
/ stands for a stressed syllable

Common rhythm patterns

Some other common rhythm patterns include the following:

- The **trochee**: two syllables, with only the first stressed, e.g. 'cauldron'

- The **anapaest**: three syllables, with only the third stressed, e.g. 'Halloween'

- The **dactyl**: one stressed syllable followed by two unstressed, e.g. 'tangerine'

- The **spondee**: two consecutive syllables that are both stressed, e.g. 'hard luck'

💡 *When reading poetry, try to read lines out loud so that you can hear the effect of the words. This makes it easier to spot the rhythm pattern.*

Key words   meter • iambic pentameter • feet

Rhythm in poetry and common rhythm patterns

1 How many syllables are there in a line of iambic pentameter? _____

2 What does meter mean? _____

3 What does trochee mean? _____

4 What does anapaest mean? _____

5 What does dactyl mean? _____

6 What does spondee mean? _____

7 What type of rhythm is 'big deal' an example of? _____

8 Read these lines of poetry. What type of rhythm do they contain?

a) *To strive, to seek, to find, and not to yield* (Tennyson)

_____

b) *With the odours of the forest* (Longfellow)

_____

c) *Be near me when my light is low* (Tennyson)

_____

d) *Half a League, Half a League, Half a League, onward* (Tennyson)

_____

9 Write your own examples of the following.

a) Write two lines of iambic pentameter.

_____

_____

b) Write a line that contains trochee.

_____

c) Write a line that contains anapaest.

_____

d) Write a line that contains dactyl.

_____

e) Write a line that contains spondee.

_____

16

Total marks   16

Genre and style

Genre

As you become a more skilled reader at Level 6 and above, you should be able to recognise features of different styles and **genres** of writing. Genre is the word given to a set of informal rules used to group together and categorise certain types of writing. There are many genres of writing. For example:

- Horror
- Action-adventure
- Fantasy
- Science fiction
- Crime
- Wild West / Western
- Comedy
- Romance

Different genres can be mixed, for example, you could have a romantic comedy, or a science fiction horror story. New genres are created when writers mix the features of existing genres.

Features of the science fiction genre

By examining one genre, it is possible to see the kinds of informal rules that go towards categorising writing in a genre. For example, this extract would be from the science fiction genre:

Zak Stone, vice-commander of the inter-galactic fleet boldly strapped on his protective gravity suit and stepped into the docking bay. The shuttle was due to take him across the Zoltanian asteroid belt towards the undiscovered planets in the Berrickian sector. Reports had been coming in to fleet headquarters about space-pirates operating in this region and he was on his way to find out.

This extract reveals itself as science fiction because of the following features:
- Character – in the science fiction genre, you would expect to find characters like space travellers.
- Setting – the extract is set in outer-space, which is common in science fiction stories.
- Description and language – science fiction often contains invented, unusual names and scientific sounding language to describe futuristic technology.
- Names – in science fiction, characters are often given unusual, futuristic names.
- **Plot** – in science fiction stories, characters often go on a journey or quest to explore the unknown.
- **Themes** and ideas – science fiction, like many action-influenced genres, often contains themes of good versus evil.

Typical features of genres

This table shows some typical features of two other popular genres:

Genre	Typical features
Horror	Spooky words, e.g. dark, creepy, shiver; ghosts, monsters; scary settings, e.g. dark, night, old buildings, forests
Action-adventure	Treasure, maps, discoveries; an explorer, the hero; exotic setting, e.g. jungle, mountains, caves.

 Knowing what genre a story belongs to will sometimes help you to predict what will happen.

Key words   genre • plot • theme

Genre

1 Read the following extracts. Which genre does each one mainly belong to?

a) *The truck rolled violently over on its side and tipped Idaho Smith out into the dusty ditch. Quickly, he picked himself up and glanced round to see the sprinting figures of two agents racing towards him. Quick as a flash, he rolled into the undergrowth and covered himself with as much foliage as he could muster. The figures trotted by, missing him completely. As soon as they disappeared round the next bend, Smith dusted himself down and leapt, monkey-like over a nearby ledge and hurtled with increasing speed towards the raging torrent of the river. There was only one way to get away – and that involved getting wet.*

_____

b) *Suzanna dreamily turned and gazed towards the rugged, masculine features of the man of her dreams. The light shone from behind him, framing his dark, handsome features. She trembled with nerves – would this be the moment when... when he asked her to marry him? She adjusted her dress and took a step towards him – her heart skipped a beat as she made her move.*

_____

c) *Edvark the elf-goblin lifted his hatchet and stepped out through the door of his hut. In the distance he could hear the rumbling of the local fire-dragon and see the sparks from its latest raid falling on the tips of the mountains. It wasn't going to be a good day for this particular elf-goblin. From his grand-elf's attic he'd found a letter on parchment – ancient parchment – from before the time of the fire-dragon, telling stories of a lost place with a mysterious, dark treasure. Edvark's curiosity was going to get him in trouble one day – and that day was today.*

_____

(3)

Typical features of genres

1 Which genre would you mainly associate with these features?

a) Space-ships, aliens, futuristic gadgets, planets, time-travel _____

b) Graveyards, vampires, spooky places, night-time, evil _____

c) Horses, gunfights, the Wild West, deserts, tumbleweed, wagons _____

d) Criminals, detectives, police, robberies, chases, money _____

e) Hearts, flowers, kisses, love, longing, desire _____

(5)

Total marks (8)

Context – Shakespeare and before

Literature before Shakespeare

When reading and writing about poetry and plays, it helps to have an understanding of the times in which they were written in order to gain a wider understanding of the writer's topics and ideas.

Here are some important periods in **Literary history**, up to and including the time of Shakespeare.

Anglo-Saxon literature
Not a great deal of Anglo-Saxon writing survives compared to other periods; stories were only being written down for the first time. Before this, many stories were told **orally**. In order to remember these story-poems, such as the famous *Beowulf*, they contained lots of alliteration and simple rhymes. These kinds of features helped to make them catchy and easy to remember.

Literature from the Middle Ages
The most famous writer in the Middle Ages was **Geoffrey Chaucer**. Chaucer wrote *The Canterbury Tales*, a collection of stories told by Pilgrims on their way to Canterbury Cathedral. Some of the stories are serious, some are very funny and some are quite rude! Chaucer's stories are important though, because as well as being entertaining, they tell us a great deal about people's lives and their attitudes and beliefs during the Middle Ages.

Another important writer in the Middle Ages was **Sir Thomas Malory**. He wrote *Le Morte d'Arthur*, a collection of stories and legends about King Arthur and the Knights of the Round Table and their search for the Holy Grail. These stories are still well-known today.

Shakespeare and his contemporaries

Regarded by many people as the golden age of English Literature, the 16th and 17th centuries produced many important writers. Shakespeare is certainly the best known; he is important because of his success in writing in a wide variety of styles and because of his huge impact on the English language – many common expressions that we use today come from his writing. Shakespeare wrote about all classes of people, from commoners to Kings, as well as people and fantasy creatures from out of this world – no-one had ever written in such a wide range of styles before.

Other important writers from this time included:
- **Ben Jonson** – he wrote plays and poetry and is said to have enjoyed debating with Shakespeare in London taverns.
- **Christopher Marlowe** – another of Shakespeare's contemporaries, he might have gone on to produce work to rival Shakespeare's, if he had not been mysteriously killed in 1593.

There was a thriving theatrical tradition in London in the late 16th century and the Globe Theatre (which has now been rebuilt) burnt down while one of Shakespeare's plays was being performed. In Elizabethan times, the first dictionary had not been written and so writers were quite used to making up words and re-arranging sentences to make their writing more exciting. Elizabethan audiences were as much used to listening to plays as they were to watching them.

Key words   Literary history • orally

Literature before Shakespeare

1 Find out three facts about each of these writers / texts.

a) The Venerable Bede _____

_____

b) *Beowulf* _____

_____

c) *Sir Gawain and the Green Knight* _____

_____

9

Shakespeare and his contemporaries

1 Find out three facts about each of these writers / texts.

a) Sir Philip Sidney _____

_____

b) Christopher Marlowe _____

_____

c) Ben Jonson _____

_____

d) Edmund Spenser _____

_____

e) John Donne _____

_____

f) William Shakespeare's sonnets _____

_____

g) William Shakespeare's plays _____

_____

_____

21

Total marks 30

Context – after Shakespeare

Reading

Learn

Literature after Shakespeare

After Shakespeare's time, there were many more developments in Literature, for example, the **novel** was invented. Before the early 18th century, novels did not exist as we know them now. The first novels were collections of letters between characters; these letters eventually changed into what we know now as **chapters**. An example of an early novel is *Pamela* by Samuel Richardson.

The Romantic poets

The **Romantics** were a group of poets including William Wordsworth, John Keats, Percy Bysshe Shelley and Samuel Taylor Coleridge. At the time, they weren't known as Romantics – that name was given to them later, when critics realised that they had several features of their writing in common.

'Romantic' does not refer to love – it refers to how the writers were inspired by nature. The Romantics were important because they introduced a new way of looking at the world and they introduced a lot of important political ideas through their poetry.

Other important writers

Jane Austen only wrote six complete novels. But she wrote many letters throughout her life and other works when she was a child. She based her novels on the types of people around her, their lives, customs and behaviour. She has remained very popular because of her keen observation of human nature, her humour and her importance in influencing other writers.

Emily, Anne and Charlotte Brontë were the surviving daughters of the Reverend Patrick Brontë. They spent a large part of their lives in Haworth in Yorkshire. Despite living in an unfashionable, isolated part of the world, they wrote passionate novels and poetry which shocked society, as they were expressing the feelings of women in a time when that was seen as inappropriate. Charlotte's *Jane Eyre* and Emily's *Wuthering Heights* both described the fierce power of love, something which readers still relate to today.

Charles Dickens wrote in a variety of forms and his work was often published in newspapers of the time. This meant that his novels were written in short parts with **cliff-hangers** between chapters, so that readers would want to buy the next edition of the newspaper. Dickens wrote a great deal about the social and political problems of his time in order to raise awareness of issues in society, such as his criticism of the legal system in his novel *Bleak House*.

Like Dickens, **John Steinbeck** wrote about social problems of his day, but he wrote about life in America. His novels *The Grapes of Wrath* and *Of Mice and Men* described the problems faced by workers affected by, or living through, the Great Depression of the 1920s and 30s.

There are many important writers. Try to read as much as you can, and try to find out something about the author's background and what inspired them to write.

Literature after Shakespeare

1 Find out three facts about each of these writers / texts.

a) William and Dorothy Wordsworth _____

_____

_____

b) Mary Shelley's *Frankenstein* _____

_____

_____

c) John Keats _____

_____

_____

d) Jane Austen's *Pride and Prejudice* _____

_____

_____

e) Jane Austen's letters _____

_____

f) Charlotte Brontë's *Jane Eyre* _____

_____

g) Emily Brontë's *Wuthering Heights* _____

_____

h) Emily Brontë's poetry _____

_____

i) Charles Dickens' *Hard Times* _____

_____

j) John Steinbeck's *Of Mice and Men* _____

_____

30

Delivering a talk or presentation

At Level 6 you will have to show greater skill in presenting your ideas through speaking. One way that you might do this is by delivering a talk or presentation.

Audience and purpose

Who is your audience?

Your audience will affect your talk in a number of ways. If you are talking to a group of friends, or people who know you, then this will allow you to be informal. If you are talking to older people, or in a formal situation, then your speech will have to be more formal. For example, if you are delivering a presentation in your science class about how to conduct an experiment, you need to be quite formal. You must also consider how much your audience knows about the subject you are talking about, because that will affect your content.

What is the purpose of your talk?

Think about what you are trying to achieve through your presentation. Are you trying to entertain, inform or perhaps even persuade your audience? This will affect what you say. For example:

- If the purpose is to entertain, then your talk might use humour, anecdotes and suitable props.
- If the purpose is to inform, then clear structure, appropriate technical vocabulary and sensible organisation will be important.
- If the purpose is to persuade, then you might need to use a range of persuasive techniques such as rhetorical questions in order to convince the audience that your ideas are correct.

Content

What are you expected to talk about?

If your audience already knows some things about your chosen topic, then do not risk boring them by repeating what they already know. You will need to research your topic carefully – do not say things that you are not sure of, because you might get asked questions about them that you cannot answer! Make some notes that you can refer to.

How long should your talk last?

You will usually be told how long your talk should last. It is important that you stick to the time you are given so make sure you practise beforehand. Break your talk into sections and time each section. When you know how long it takes overall, adjust the length of individual sections, rather than trying to adjust the whole presentation.

What facilities will you have to deliver your talk?

If you are able to use an interactive whiteboard, make sure you do not read off the screen – your audience can hopefully do that without you doing it for them. Instead, talk about the slides you use and add extra information. Use pictures rather than too much text; pick out details of the images and use them to develop your ideas. If you are not using an interactive white board, then use cue cards – but do not read directly off them. Bring in props and talk about them to support your ideas. This will help to keep the audience's attention.

Key words   anecdote • rhetorical question • cue cards

Audience, purpose and content

1 a) i) You are going to see if you can talk for one minute, without detailed notes, about your favourite television programme. In order to help you, there are six prompts below. Try to talk for about 10 seconds on each prompt. Time yourself.

- What it is about.
- Your favourite episode.
- Your favourite character.
- What you hope will happen in it.
- What you dislike about it.
- Why you would recommend it to other people.

ii) Write the total time for your first attempt here. _____

b) i) Now try again, but this time, think about how far you got through the prompts and how long you took. If you went over time, reduce the time you spent speaking on some of the sections. If you did not speak for long enough, try to increase the amount of time you spend on each section.

ii) Write the total time for your second attempt here. _____

2 Choose a topic of your own choice. Write six, one-word prompts in the spaces below and then repeat the exercise above. This will help you practise planning a talk and then presenting it without relying on detailed notes.

- _____
- _____
- _____
- _____
- _____
- _____

3 Choose a photograph, which does not have any text on it. Label six things in the photograph. Try to talk for one minute about the photograph, without repeating yourself, using only your labels as notes. This will help you to practise giving a talk without reading off a script. Write your labels in the spaces below.

- _____
- _____
- _____
- _____
- _____
- _____

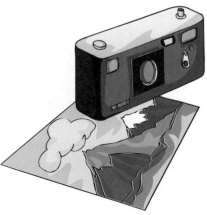

16

Total marks 16

Listening and making notes

Listening

Listening is perhaps a more important skill in some ways than speaking, because listening is how we learn. But listening is one thing – **remembering** is another, so it is important to make good notes to help you to remember what you have heard.

Making good notes

The following stages will take you through how to make good notes.

1 Put a title and date on your notes – this will help you to remember when you made the notes and where they come in your work. If you have lots of pieces of paper to sort through and organise, then dates and titles will be invaluable.

2 Do not limit the length of your notes – you can always sort and shorten them afterwards and this will help you to remember what you have written.

3 Leave spaces between your notes – this means that you will be able to add extra comments and detail if you need to, later on, without having to write using small handwriting.

4 When making the notes as you are listening, it will probably be easier to use one colour of pen, as it will take time to swap over pens and colours and you might miss something important. When you revisit and tidy up your notes, you might then wish to colour-code them.

5 Make lists, spider diagrams or charts as you write. This will help you to organise your ideas.

6 Do not write everything in full. Use single words or phrases wherever it is appropriate to do so. Unless you are making notes for someone else, then the only person who needs to understand your notes is you, so as long as you can understand what you have written, your writing is fine. But make sure that you will understand your notes later on.

Always be ready to make notes – make sure you carry spare pens and a small pad of paper.

Key words   spider diagram

Listening and making good notes

1 Watch, or listen to, the news on television or radio. Make notes and then complete the questions below.

a) What date was the news broadcast? _____

b) Write down the first three main stories in the broadcast, in the order in which they were delivered, and then write a brief summary of each one. Your summaries do not have to be in full sentences.

Story 1
i) What was it about?

_____

ii) Summary:

_____

_____

_____

Story 2
i) What was it about?

_____

ii) Summary:

_____

_____

_____

Story 3
i) What was it about?

_____

ii) Summary:

_____

_____

_____

c) Using just your notes, explain these three news stories to a friend or relative in as much detail as possible. (Explaining your notes to someone else is also a good way to remember them.)

8

Speaking and listening

Total marks   8

Expression and body language

Effective speaking

When speaking, you need to be aware that it is not just *what* you say, but *how* you say it and your body language that has an effect on the audience. Effective speakers can deliberately control their expression and body language for effect – it can be planned and practised to improve communication skills.

Expression

Expression in speech depends on what effect the speaker wants to create. Volume can go up and down and pauses and tone can be changed.

There are no hard and fast rules; the best approach is to plan what you want to say and practise. If you have a script that you need to follow, then you could annotate the script with the places where you want to change expression or pause.

Eye contact

Eye contact with your audience is very important. If you do not look at the people you are speaking to, you will not be able to engage their interest or even their attention.

The way to develop good eye contact is to choose points in your notes where you will look up at the audience, for example, at the end of a sentence, section or paragraph. Another way of creating better eye contact is to learn your notes off by heart.

Non-verbal cues

Non-verbal cues are things that you might do in order to reinforce or support what you are saying, for example:

- Pounding the table or your fist – this might add emphasis to the most important points
- Pointing – this again might add emphasis to a point, or could be used as a way of engaging with someone in the audience to reinforce a rhetorical question such as 'Would you do that?'
- Folding your arms – this could suggest that you are firm in your ideas if you do it deliberately at a key moment. If you do it all the way through a talk, it may suggest that you are insecure and defensive.
- Nodding your head – this reinforces an idea that you are putting forward.
- Shrugging your shoulders – this might suggest surprise or shock at an idea.

Try to practise in front of a mirror, or with friends who you feel comfortable with, to try to make your expression and body language as natural as possible. The more you practise, the more relaxed and effective you will become.

Key words   body language • annotate • non-verbal cues

Effective speaking and non-verbal cues

1 a) Below is a short speech to prepare. Mark on the speech the places where you might use the following expression, body language techniques and non-verbal cues. You can mark them on the speech in as many places as you feel necessary. You might find it easiest to colour-code the speech in order to distinguish between the different techniques.

Technique	Colour
1. Pound the table for emphasis.	
2. Shrug your shoulders.	
3. Raise volume to emphasise a point.	
4. Pause after a rhetorical question.	
5. Look up and make eye-contact.	
6. Point	
7. Lower volume to get the audience to listen carefully.	

Speech

Boys and girls, I am speaking to you today to talk about not one, not two, but three important things.

Firstly, there is the alarming issue of litter in the school playground. It's disgusting! When are students at this school going to start taking responsibility and put their litter in the bins provided? Can you honestly say that you always do that?

Secondly – and leading on from that, there is the matter of the vending machines on the corridors. They must go. I know that people will say that they are a great facility and a fund-raiser for the school, but the amount of problems that they create is ridiculous! Litter! Students late for lessons! Mess!

And finally, I want you to think for a moment. We are an eco-school. We should be recycling our litter. Do we do this? Do we do our bit in helping to save the planet? I don't think we do enough.

b) When you have annotated the speech, practise delivering it, either in front of a mirror or to someone you know well. Do you come across as natural? If not, alter your expression, body language and non-verbal cues and try again. Carry on doing this until you are happy with your performance.

10

Glossary

Adjective – a word or phrase that describes a noun.

Adverb – a word or phrase that describes a verb.

Alliteration – a phrase where most or all of the words begin with the same sound.

Anecdote – a short account of a personal experience.

Annotate – to make notes.

Anti-climax – follows the climax; a contrast to the climax.

Apostrophe of omission – an apostrophe used to show that one or more letters are missing, e.g. can't, didn't.

Apostrophe of possession – an apostrophe used to show that something belongs to someone / something.

Assonance – the repetition of similar vowel sounds in a sentence.

Audience – the people who will be reading your writing or listening to your talk.

Bias – an influence that sways opinion.

Body language – the way the body is used during communication.

Class – the group of words to which a word belongs, e.g. nouns, adjectives, verbs, adverbs.

Cliché – a phrase or expression that has been very overused.

Cliff-hanger – a technique used in writing that ends a chapter / section in an interesting or exciting way to try to make the reader want to read on.

Climax – the most exciting / interesting point in the writing.

Colon – a punctuation mark that can be used to introduce explanations, lists or speech.

Command – an imperative, a way of using verbs to give an order or instruction, e.g. Turn left.

Complex sentence – a sentence that contains a main clause and a subordinate clause.

Connective – a word or phrase used to join sentences or paragraphs.

Consonance – the repetition of similar consonant sounds in a sentence.

Consonant – any letter of the alphabet except the vowels a, e, i, o and u.

Context – the overall setting / positioning of words in a piece of writing.

Contraction – when words are shortened, or two words are joined, by removing letters and replacing with an apostrophe.

Contrast – differences that are shown when things are compared.

Cross-reference – referencing one piece of writing to another.

Cue cards – brief notes to use as prompts when giving a talk or presentation.

Ellipsis – a sentence that is left unfinished, often used to create suspense.

Feet – sets of stressed and unstressed syllables that create a rhythm pattern.

Formal – the conventional use of language in a standard form.

Genre – the category of style that a piece of writing falls into.

Hyperbole – exaggeration.

Iambic pentameter – a meter used in poetry; there are ten syllables (alternating unstressed, stressed) in a line.

Imagery – words used to build up a picture in a piece of writing.

Imperative – a command, a way of using verbs to give an order or instruction, e.g. Turn left.

Informal – the way language is used when speaking / writing to friends / relatives. It probably contains non-standard grammar and slang.

Internal rhyme – rhyme within a line.

Juxtaposition – the positioning of two contrasting words, phrases or ideas next to or near each other.

Limerick – a five-line poem which has the rhyme pattern AABBA.

Literary history – the history of literature (plays, poetry, stories, novels).

Main clause – the main part of a sentence which makes sense on its own.

Metaphor – where a writer describes something as if it were something else.

Meter – poetic rhythm which is determined by the arrangement of syllables in patterns.

Mnemonic – a technique (e.g. a rhyme or acronym) used to help memorise something.

Mood – the overall feel of the writing, e.g. sad, angry, happy, excited.

Non-verbal cues – actions that might be used to emphasise points made during a presentation.

Noun – a word that names an object or feeling.

Novel – a collection of chapters that make up a story.

Onomatopoeia – when a word sounds like the noise it describes, e.g. crash, shatter.

Orally – spoken (as opposed to written).

Oxymoron – two contradictory terms placed together, e.g. 'bitter sweet'.

Passive voice – a sentence where it is not always clear who or what does the action, e.g. The boy was chased.

Pathetic fallacy – a writing technique in which human feelings are used to describe non-human things.

Personification – a writing technique in which human characteristics are used to describe non-human things.

Phoneme – the smallest individual sounds in a word.

Plot – the structure of the story, what happens.

Plural – more than one.

Prefix – letters added to the beginning of a word to alter its meaning.